HOW TO
SATISFACT
NEW YORK STYLE

- How to get an apartment in New York *without* a fee
- The 10 worst cab drivers in all of the city
- How to get a parking ticket dismissed
- Making a Big Stink: getting satisfaction when your complaint gets ignored
- How to get a noisy neighbor off your back and qualify for a rent reduction
- Where to get a lawyer for nothing
- The worst fast foods you can eat and their fat content
- The *new* top 10 rip-off businesses in NYC
- The biggest mistake people commit in Small Claims
- What store you should *never* shop in
- The 6 best 'spare change' lines
- NYC legislators with the worst attendance records
- The 10 worst tourist trap electronic stores
- Hospital emergency rooms and shortest waiting times
- How to roach-proof your apartment
- 16 proven tactics to avoid getting mugged
- Bus routes with the worst on-time performance
- How you can keep your pet despite what the lease says
- Cheapest garages to park your car in
- 3 subway stations you're most likely to meet a thief
- Foreign embassies with the most unpaid parking tickets
- *Plus much much more*

...AND THE MOST *EFFECTIVE* WAYS TO REGISTER YOUR COMPLAINT AND FIGHT BACK!

COMPLETE WITH ALL NEW PHONE NUMBERS!

GET-A-GRIP NEW YORK BOOK II

HOW TO GET SATISFACTION WITH THE BIGGEST HASSLES

RAYMOND ALVIN

© Copyright 1997
Get-A-Grip New York - Book II
by Raymond Alvin - All rights reserved
Formerly titled: *The NYC Get-A-Grip Gripe Book* ©

ISBN # 0-9644961-3-5
Second Edition/ Second Printing, Completely Revised

The author and publisher disclaim any liability with the
use of this information.

All rights reserved. No part of this book may be
reproduced, stored in a retrieval system, transmitted in any
form or by any means, electronic, mechanical,
photocopied or otherwise without the written permission
of the publisher, except for the inclusion of brief
quotations in a review.

Library of Congress Cataloging-in-Publication Date

©

STREETBEAT PUBLICATIONS
P.O. Box 32 - Ansonia Station
New York, New York 10023-0032

Cover: Oscar Gonzalez Design

CONTENTS

PART TWO
I Can't Hear Myself Scream & Other Irritants

PART THREE
Don't You Hate It When That Happens?

MY KINDA TOWN

In New York it's not the heat -- it's the insanity.

Ming Toy

A city of tough damaged people and right angles.

Pete Hamill

Practicing therapy in New York is like selling Band-Aids at Custer's last stand.

Ellen Orchid, Psychiatrist

Everybody in LA is so friendly, just to feel back home in New York -- I gave myself the finger three times.

David Letterman

I moved to New York City for my health -- I'm paranoid and it was the only place where my fears were justified.

Anita Weiss

I like it here in New York. I like the idea of having to keep eyes in the back of your head all the time.

John Cale

New York is the only city in the world where you can be awakened by a smell.

Jeff Garland

The only real advantage of New York is that all of its inhabitants ascend to heaven right after their deaths, having served their full term in hell.

Barnard College Bulletin

There is no human reason to be here -- except for the sheer ecstasy of being crowded together.

Jean Baudrilland

The faces in New York remind me of people who played a game and lost.

Murray Kempton

Living in New York is like being at some terrible late-night party. You're tired -- you've had a headache since you arrived -- but you can't leave because then you'd miss the party.

Simon Haggart

It's hard to think of the immortal soul when you take the subway twice a day.

Anonymous

According to a recent survey, the three most common phrases heard in New York are...

1. Hey Taxi!
2. Which way is it to Bloomingdales?
3. Don't worry, it's only a flesh wound.

David Letterman

In Rome I am weighed down by a lack of momentum, the inertia of a spent civilization. In New York I feel plugged into a strong alternating current of hope and despair.

Ted Morgan

In New York you can see what flies up your nose.

Milt Kamen

ACKNOWLEDGMENTS

Thanks to the hundreds of individuals, city agencies and bureaucrats who have contributed their time and expertise in explaining how things work and sharing their problem-solving techniques. My special thanks to Matthew Clark for his unique observations, insights and invaluable assistance.

TO THE READER

This book is a source for protecting your rights as a resident or visitor to New York City. It is a know-your-rights and get satisfaction guide.

The information contained in this book is true. Every effort has been made to bring you the most current, up-to-date information in New York City. If a telephone number has changed, hang in there. You can always get the new number by dialing directory assistance or the *New York City Agency Information Line* at 788-4636.

If you are having trouble getting through to a city hotline alternative numbers are provided.

Phone numbers are subject to change. Unless otherwise noted, all phones numbers are 212 area code. The mentioning of any business in this book is not an endorsement.

"It's not how deep you fish,
It's how you wiggle your worm."

Anon

"Life is a losing game,
and you might as well enjoy it."

Harold Clurman

"Sometimes you're the bird,
sometimes you're the windshield."

Bag lady in Times Square

For Zeke
who helped me get through most of it

NEW YORK CITY: HEARTBURN CAPITAL OF THE WORLD

Recently a study was conducted by New York Hospital-Cornell Medical Center on the subject of acid indigestion. The study went on to say that stress is linked to heartburn and revealed that a disproportionate amount of heartburn sufferers are right here in New York City. Did the study come as a surprise to those of us who live and work here? Nah. Heartburn, stress and getting pissed off are just part and parcel of being in the world's greatest city.

In fact one of the more effective ways of meeting people in New York is to start up a conversation with a stranger and discover that the subject of complaining proves successful. It is very often a shared topic and establishes a common ground. One guy at a party started off by talking about how bad traffic was in the city. He soon met the woman of his dreams when she started to complain about how the subway had begun to stink. They were made for each other. Everybody in New York City complains at one time or another. For some, this is the city they just love to hate.

All in all, New York can be one grumpy town. Often what makes this town so exhilarating is what makes it oppressive. Traditionally New Yorkers have never been known to be a happy lot. But they can give the rest of the civilized world lessons on stamina and true grit in the face of adversity.

The message that prevails in these chapters is not what an unfit place New York is to live in but how to get leverage and complain effectively when you do have a gripe.

As I've said before, in New York we don't call them water main breaks, unattended car alarms and muggings. We call them "character-building experiences." *New York City* and *Quality of Life* are a boa constrictor and a mongoose.

Having spent practically all my life here, I 'd say with a fair amount of certainty, that the major difference between those of us who live here and the rest of the world -- is that we New Yorkers *expect* to be shit upon on a daily basis. People who live here know that they're going to get hassled, jerked around and be on the receiving end of a major attitude. It's all a matter of when and by whom. Folks who haven't come to this realization yet can be spotted grinning at nothing in particular right before they step into a pile of dog poop.

According to a survey put out by the US Department of Consumer Affairs, only 30% of people bother to complain at all. Yet one complaint might be the one to break the camel's back. As a New Yorker it is your constitutional right to complain. It helps vent your anger and frustration. Trouble is most of the time you do it to the dog or to someone who can do you absolutely no good. That's why the necessity for this book.

I'm sure that I've made just about every mistake in this city that's possible so I can tell you that I'm not speaking from some divine state of perfection. But I have learned from my mistakes. If I can save you at least one tenth the hassles I've had to endure, I'll consider this venture a success.

Here, you will read about getting satisfaction and attention from those who have not only gone the route and prevailed, but those on the inside who share a wealth of information on not only getting a grip but making life more manageable in New York City.

As was said once before, "the meek shall inherit the earth - but they sure as hell won't get what they want in New York City."

Raymond Alvin
The Original Mad as Hell New Yawker

"I'm appalled that we, the public, resign ourselves to the level of service that we get and we don't take action on a more frequent basis until something devastating happens."

A New Yorker

SOME REVEALING FACTS ON COMPLAINING

- Most people don't know how or where to complain and get results that work. If they do complain, they invariably do so to a person who can do them no good.

- A good many people feel they'll be labeled a troublemaker for insisting on their rights. They feel "the system" is corrupt and that nothing is likely to change.

- It is the young who are more likely to complain than the old. Those with higher incomes are more likely to complain.

- Most folks don't know how or where to get satisfaction nor what to do with their rage. They hate to write letters because they fear it won't be perfect at first glance.

- Many times the rationale is, "what good will my one complaint do"? This even though one complaint might just be the one among many to tip the scales in your favor.

- By *not* complaining about something that is wrong, the message you're sending to those in positions of authority is that everything's okay.

- You don't have to pay or seek out lawyers to settle your grievances. You'd be surprised what one person can accomplish.

- Cumulative complaints help clean up the mess. On a grand scale it helped end the Vietnam war and forced two presidents from office.

- Most folks think that complaining will be so time-consuming that the problem won't even be worth it.

- Maybe the Rolling Stones couldn't get any satisfaction, but *you* can!

Source: Consumer Complaint Handling in America study conducted by the US Office of Consumer Affairs

HOW TO *KVETCH* (COMPLAIN) EFFECTIVELY

☛ Remember to get the name of the person you are talking to at the outset of the conversation.

☛ If at all possible, try to resolve the complaint with the other party *before* going to a third party.

☛ Don't waste your time complaining to a subordinate who does not set policy. Go up the chain of command.

☛ If you go to a state or federal agency, you stand a very good chance of having your complaint resolved.

☞ Be polite and courteous when you deal with an agency. By doing so you're more apt to get positive results. You must remember to follow up due to the large number of complaints received. The whole idea is to help stack the odds better in your favor.

☞ Attitude is key. Even though you may be boiling mad, don't take it out on the agency that is there to assist you in the process.

☞ State your problem in simple terms. You must make the complaint palatable for the person on the other end. Don't put off the person who is trying to help you.

☞ Make sure you thank the other person for their time by sending a thank-you note. By doing so you are keeping the process open to others and to yourself should you have a future difficulty.

☞ Be persistent. If at first you don't get the response you desire, don't quit and above all, keep reading this book.

THE LITTLE SQUIRREL THAT COULD

Recently I read about the story of a mishap in Bristol, Connecticut. It seems on a recent Thanksgiving day a squirrel jumped across power lines causing them to fall and short. More than 11,000 customers lost power. Many of the residents had to resort to backyard grills to cook their dinner.

The actions of this one squirrel, who had absolutely no idea the power he possessed was astounding.

It led me to think that if just one squirrel could do all that without thinking -- imagine the power of just one person.

PART ONE

STREET SMARTS

#1　　TIPS FOR TOURISTS

HOW TO SHOP STREET VENDORS

- ☹ Don't accept their price the first time around.
- ☹ Always remember to haggle.
- ☹ Don't buy shrink wrapped items on the street, as they prove to be either defective or refurbished and passed off as brand new.
- ☹ A good deal of the time counterfeit goods are sold. Some examples of this are Seiko and Cartier watches, Ralph Lauren and Lacoste polo shirts

HOW TO HAGGLE FOR THE BEST PRICE

A study conducted by Money Magazine reports that most anything is negotiable. The more time a salesperson talks to you, the more their investment in you. Be friendly. Establish a connection with the salesperson and win their trust. Lastly, have a price in mind when negotiating.

Get A Grip: Don't waste your time haggling with a salesperson who doesn't have the authority and needs to check with his boss for every procedure. Go to the power source. When in a department store - ask if and when the item is going on sale.

Average mark up rates for dealers: clothing 100%, small appliances 30%, large appliances 15%, automobiles 5-10%

NEW YORK FUN FACT

Counterfeit watches and other phony name brand merchandise are often sold on the streets of New York. Never buy shrink wrapped or any other merchandise you cannot examine. Chances are it's defective and you won't know until after the fact. Remember to bargain and do so quietly so that your price doesn't go public. If you're not satisfied, walk away. Usually the vendor will stop you from leaving.

#2

GETTING YOUR MONEY BACK
& THE NEW TOP 10
RIP-OFF BUSINESSES IN NEW YORK

Jeanette Chapman was whopping mad. She had just hired a moving company to transport her furniture and belongings to a new residence in Astoria, Queens. Everything had gone smoothly during the move. Nothing was broken and everything proved to be on schedule. The furniture arrived in Astoria and as a preliminary step the movers unloaded all of her possessions on the sidewalk.

The trouble started when the movers found out that Chapman had no intention of tipping any of them. Consequently all of her belongings remained on the sidewalk as the moving company bid her a fond farewell. The angry consumer called the Better Business Bureau to complain. She also notified the Department of Transportation, after discovering that this type of complaint does not fall under the jurisdiction of the Department of Consumer Affairs.

But Chapman didn't stop there. She started her own newsletter and distributed copies warning anybody who would listen to avoid doing business with a certain moving company. While she never got the company back to move her furniture off the sidewalk she got the ultimate revenge -- she told her story and became what most businesses have learned to fear -- a dissatisfied customer who sought satisfaction.

While the circumstances may be a bit out of the ordinary, the Better Business Bureau (a private non-profit agency) receives about 40,000 complaints annually according to Jerry DeSantos, Director of Information at the Bureau. "We do get restitution for 2 out of 3 people who complain to us," he said. "The only types of complaints we don't handle involve malpractice, landlord-tenant, employer-employee and monies that haven't been collected for services rendered."

The Department of Consumer Affairs, another complaint-driven agency but city-operated, claims to have saved consumers $1,291,407 in restitution just for 1996. However, not all businesses are regulated by the DCA.

Some of the exceptions along with their regulatory bodies are:

- *Moving companies,* The Dept. Of Transportation,
  718-482-4816
- *Auto repair,* Dept. of Motor Vehicles,   645-5550
- Complaints with *Doctors,* Dept. of Health,
  div. of Professional Medical Conduct   613-2650
- *Other Professionals,* Dept. Education,
  div. Professional Discipline,   800-442-8106
- *Banking* complaints, NYS Banking Dept.,   618-6642

For a comparative listing of credit card rates, fees and grace periods, call the NYS Banking Dept.
  800-518-8866
- To find out about the best credit cards   800-344-7714
Consumer Information Line - Card Track

   To help stack the odds in your favor, the DCA recommends taking some preliminary steps before bringing in outside agencies:

1. Try to resolve the matter with the merchant. You can save yourself a good deal of time by trying to work out things together. If it was a purchase by credit card, call your Visa, MasterCard or Amex office and dispute the amount of the transaction. You won't be responsible for the interest while it's being disputed.

2. After you've written to your credit card company, send a copy of the letter to the merchant.

3. Write the business directly. List the reasons for dispute. Be sure to tell the merchant what it is you want from them. Sarcasm and anger are usually counter-productive to the situation.

4. If you either receive an unsatisfactory answer or no answer, contact the DCA and explain what has transpired. Get ready to submit any evidence (i.e. receipts, correspondence, contracts, etc.) along with your complaint.

5. As a precautionary measure, avoid paying substantial amounts in cash. Always ask for an itemized receipt and warranty.

TOP 10 WORST ELECTRONIC STORES AS RATED BY THE DEPARTMENT OF CONSUMER AFFAIRS

Some of the most common consumer complaints are ones that involve overcharging by electronics stores randomly located between 34th and 59th streets from Lexington to Eighth avenues. Here are some to avoid doing business with;

VIOLATOR	ADDRESS		VIOLATIONS
Marquis Galleries	519 Lexington		102
47th St Audio/Photo	520 Fifth Ave		89
Fordham Electronics	66 E. Fordham Rd	Bronx	85
Golden Temple	885 6th Ave		77
Rainbow Camera	875 6th Ave		76
7th Avenue Gallery	162 West 56th St		72
West Side Camera	694 8th Ave		72
Electronic Wonders	485 Fifth Ave		68
Audio Photo Intl	5 West 42nd St		62
Eastern Computer	425 Madison Ave		48

Note: Watch out for refurbished second hand merchandise that is repackaged and sold as new, offering items for sale above the Manufacturer's Suggested Retail Price without disclosure and "gray market items" which are accessories that come with a unit but are sold separately.

GET A GRIP

If you're not getting any satisfaction with all your efforts, follow these steps:

- Call 212-487-4398, the DCA general complaint line where you will eventually speak with a representative. As with most municipalities, expect to be on the phone for some time. Don't expect just to whiz through the process.

- The rep will first screen you to determine whether their agency can help you. If so, a form will be mailed to you so you can list exactly what happened. You may also visit the nearest DCA office in order to facilitate matters (see end of chapter for locations and key numbers.)

- Once you do receive the complaint form and send it back, it will take about 15 days before the case gets assigned a number and is filed. From that point, it will take about two months before a mediator gets assigned to your case.

- A licensed business gives the DCA more leverage, and the city agency has the power to padlock any business that repeatedly breaks the law.

THE TRUTH ABOUT
GOING OUT OF BUSINESS SALES

New York City law *(Administrative code, Chapter 32, title B, article 28, "Sales")* states that a store claiming to go out of business must obtain a special license from the DCA and must go out of business within 90 days. If they don't, they risk a $100 fine every day that they remain open. Enough ignored summonses can spell "shut down" for a business. Next comes a *"Padlock Citation,"* which closes down the business.

AN OUNCE OF PREVENTION
IS WORTH A POUND OF *TSURIS**
(*AGGRAVATION)

☞ The DCA claims to have an 82% success rate in the favor of the consumer by way of either refund, exchange, or replacement. Before you make a purchase, the best advice is to shop around. More than likely you will find it cheaper elsewhere. Be aware of any store refund policy. That policy *must* be displayed where sales transactions take place. If not, it is a violation of consumer protection law. Not all establishments choose to refund money.

☞ Know the product. Do your homework. Be familiar with the different features and see if the salesperson knows what they're talking about.

☞ Call the DCA and find out if the store you're about to do business with is licensed (487-4379). In situations where you are about to spend a substantial amount of money, call the BBB to see what kind of rating the establishment received from the bureau, *i.e. satisfactory, unsatisfactory or no rating.*

While a business may evade the law for a while, the DCA makes periodic sweeps of violators after monitoring a business in question.   According to sources, the law (which dates back over sixty years) is only periodically enforced. A business with its special *"going out of business"* license is not permitted to order any new merchandise.

WHAT TO DO WITH YOUR RAGE

If you feel you have a justified complaint and a nagging suspicion that you've been wronged -- contact your local Department of Consumer Affairs and Better Business Bureau but don't stop there if you don't get satisfaction. Check out the *Big Stink* chapter (Pg. 252) for more attention-getting strategies..

MANHATTAN	42 Broadway	9th fl	212-487-4398
QUEENS	120-55 Queens Blvd. Kew Gardens	Room 301A	718-286-2990
STATEN ISL.	10 Richmond Terrace Boro Hall	Room 422	718-816-2280

THE BAIT AND SWITCH SCAM

This practice has been going on for decades. The way it works is: you go after an advertised special at the store. The salesperson tells you that they're temporarily out of stock and offers you another model "just as good."

He then mentions that he can save you some bucks in the process. Next, he persuades you to buy the different model bearing a close resemblance to the product (what he didn't tell you is that its last year's model.) Instead of saving $10, it should have been $50 less than the newer model.

COUNTERING

Go shopping with a specific model number of the unit you want to purchase. Being prepared before buy. If they're suddenly out of stock on your item, request a rain check.

CUSTOMER SATISFACTION

Every day for three weeks, a man who recently bought an Oldsmobile parked his car right outside the General Motors building at 59th Street and Fifth Avenue. Seems he had the misfortune of owning the car less than 6 months when he discovered that his new auto needed more and more repairs. When the car dealer turned a deaf ear, the disgruntled customer decided to fasten a large sign to the hood of his car with the words, "THIS CAR IS A LEMON" and went on to list the reasons why. Located directly across the street from the Plaza Hotel, the GM building is in one of the busiest areas of the city. Lunch hour patrons would gather around the vehicle which was now the center of attention. In an effort to avoid further embarrassment the car manufacturer finally arranged to have the automobile replaced with a new one.

NYC BETTER BUSINESS BUREAU'S
TOP 10
MOST FREQUENTLY COMPLAINED ABOUT
INDUSTRIES

Industry	*Complaints*
10. Health and Beauty	470
9. Moving and Storage	657
8. Travel	725
7. Publishing	851
6. Financial Services	1,162
5. Consumer Electronics	1,295
4. Home Improvement	1,452
3. Household and Office Furnishings	1,565
2. Automotive	2,027
1. Mail Order	4,025

Source: BBB - year-end totals 1995

NYC DEPARTMENT OF CONSUMER AFFAIRS
TOP 10 FREQUENTLY COMPLAINED ABOUT
BUSINESSES

Business	_Complaints_
10. Travel Agencies	178
9. Wearing Apparel	195
8. Garages & Parking Lots	261
7. TV & Radio Repair	334
6. Debt Collectors	369
5. Tow Companies	375
4. Used Car Dealers	448
3. Electronic Stores	576
2. Furniture Stores	784
1. Home Improvement Contractors	941

*Source: The Department of Consumer Affairs,
July, 1994--June 1995*

THE URBAN
GUERRILLA

If you feel like you've been wronged by a place of business why not start your own flyer or newsletter and spread the word? Computer companies have laid it all out for you via user friendly software so all you need to do is distribute it once its done.

KEY NUMBERS

- *Better Business Bureau Complaint Line*
257 Park Ave South, New York, NY 10010   533-6200
($3.80 for up to 3 listings of companies,
if you choose to write in there is no charge.)
    E-Mail address for complaints is bbb.org/bbb

- *Department of Consumer Affairs*   487-4398

IF THE ABOVE HOTLINE PROVES TO BE COLD...

- *Commissioner Dept. of Consumer Affairs*   487-4401

- *Attorney General's Office*   416-8000
120 Broadway, NYC 10271

- *NYS Consumer Protection Board*   417-4908

- *Public Citizen*
1600 20th St. NW - Washington, DC 20009
    (Founded by Ralph Nader, this organization is the
    consumer's eyes and ears in Washington.)

NEW YORK FUN FACT

Between July 1990 and November 1995, the Department of
Consumer Affairs registered over 42,112 complaints & solved
more 35,872 of them -- saving consumers over 6 million dollars.

Top Complaint-Getters

New York businesses with
the largest volume of complaints

☹ Guildwood Direct LTD. (Sweepstakes)
☹ Direct Marketing Enterprises (Direct Mail)
☹ Aristar Calendar Co. (Modeling Contest)
☹ Model Search America (Modeling)
☹ Financial Planning Assoc. (Work-at-Home)
☹ Manhattan Model Search (Modeling)
☹ Clearing House Publications (Work-At-Home)
☹ National Talent Associates (Modeling)
☹ Moishie's Moving (Moving)
☹ Teleservice One (Telemarketing)
☹ Reader's Digest
☹ Jennifer Convertibles
☹ Info Access Inc.
☹ Time Warner
☹ Citibank N.A.
☹ Giant Carpet
☹ Chemical Bank
☹ Seaman Furniture Co.
☹ American Express Co.

Source: Better Business Bureau, 1995-6

#3

CRAZY CABBIES

Best request for directions by a New York City cab driver:

A passenger boarded a taxi at Lexington & 42nd. He told the driver that he wanted to go to Lexington & 25th: The cabbie responded by saying "How would you like me to go, sir?"

Cabbie Sung Min, was cited as being one of the worst cab drivers in all of New York City according to the Taxi and Limousine Commission. He knew how to strike fear into the hearts of one out of town couple. Seems Min thought he was cut off while traveling through Central Park. He began his 'ride from hell' when he stayed on their bumper, chased them and tried to force them off the road. When the couple finally parked their car and got out, Min pulled his cab in front of them, got out a tire iron and went running after them.

The couple hid in their car cowering beneath the seats and screaming for 911.

Cabbie Raymond Colucci looked like somebody's uncle or grandfather. Colucci was a real pro according to Eugene Rodriquez, of the Taxi and Limousine Commission. "He seemed like a sweetheart of a guy," said Rodriquez. When one passenger gave him a $5 bill for a $3 fare, he would turn around and tell them they only gave them a dollar and handed it back. The passenger, rushed for time, now gave him a $10 bill. Colucci handed her back 6 bucks after she told him to keep a buck. A $3 cab ride amounted to $8.

The passenger complained to the Taxi & Limousine Commission and the administrative judge found Mr. Colucci guilty of swindling her. It turned out that he racked up a total of 19 violations from 1991-1995. Altogether Colucci had been driving a cab for some 20 years, there's no telling how many passengers he conned. He preyed mostly on tourists and earned the dubious distinction as being the bottom of the barrel when his own union reported him.

The former Chairman of the TLC, Christopher Lynn admitted in an interview that Colucci's scam was "to sound like the calmest, most rational man." But he was stealing money from passengers every day he drove a cab by overcharging them. What finally did Mr. Colucci in, was that people complained. What kept him in business was that most passengers would keep silent or not show up at hearings.

New York City cabbies (of which 5% drive with invalid licenses) are largely immigrants from Eastern Europe, Asia, Africa, and the Caribbean. In fact 89% of all New York cabbies are foreign born. Some may not know their way around the city all that well, while others race and swerve.

Getting to your destination in New York City can be a production in itself especially if you're in a hurry. You can take the subway, walk, or if you're in a more adventurous mood, take one of the city's 11,787 taxi cabs with 400 more on the way for the first time since 1937.

According to one recent survey, a cab driver is 45 times more likely to get shot than a NYC police officer. Cab drivers are victims of crime more often than any other commercial group in the city even though 80% of cab crimes involve livery and gypsy cab drivers, according to the NYPD.

It should be noted that livery cabs are permitted to pick up passengers who have called for them, not go after fares on the street (but they often do anyway). Livery cabs are licensed by the city while gypsy cabs are not.

Like any other profession, there are good cab drivers and lousy ones. What to do if you meet a real dirtbag who won't follow your directions, lower his short wave, or who takes you on the long scenic tour of hell?

GET A GRIP

- Always request a receipt. You never know when you might have a complaint or left something behind. The receipt lists the taxi's medallion number.

- These days, if you're having a problem with a NYC cab driver call 302-TAXI (9 a.m. - 5 p.m.) and speak to the Taxi & Limousine Commission, the city's licenser for taxis. The system has now been revamped so that you can speak into either voice mail or get connected to a representative. Be prepared to give specific information that includes all the particulars including: time, date, location, and incident.

- In order to speed up the process, the TLC will schedule your hearing in approximately 2-3 weeks.

- You should have the driver's name and license number, made up of 6 digits. This information can be found on the lower right-hand part of the dashboard next to the medallion number. The medallion number is also on the back of the front seat and on the roof light.

- A hearing, will be scheduled with the driver present, that you must attend. TLC headquarters is located at 221 West 41st Street. A decision is rendered on the spot by a judge and a fine may be imposed on the driver ranging anywhere from $25 to $500.

- Your identity does not have to be revealed to the driver.

TLC complaints against cabbies fall into 3 categories:
- 1/3   driving unsafely.
- 1/3   overcharging.
- 1/3   not being picked up because of race or wanting to go to the outer boroughs.

There have been cases in which some cabbies go to the trouble of installing electronic switches that make their meter run faster. Others have figured out that using smaller tires on their vehicles produces more rotations over the same distance, thus registering higher fares on the meter.

According to the TLC, and using twenty blocks to a mile, as an estimate the meter should click approximately once every four blocks traveling north to south. The blocks going from east to west in Manhattan are usually double the distance, so figure one click per block here. If you're getting a faster series of clicks on the meter, ask for a receipt and file a complaint.

As a guideline, recent citywide figures indicated that in 1994 about 12,000 people called the TLC to complain but only 6,000 returned the then required questionnaire. Out of that, another 3,000 opted for a hearing and only 1200 showed up for one.

A driver can have his license revoked if he's guilty of 3 offenses. An offense is made up of overcharging and/or refusing to take you somewhere or just one instance of overcharging by ten dollars or more. In 1995, taxi riders received $10,640 worth of restitution just by complaining.

According to a TLC survey, 1 out of every 5 passengers doesn't get to go where they want to. Many drivers refuse to make trips to the outer boroughs because they won't get a fare coming back to Manhattan. However, once you're inside the taxi, the driver must take you where you want to go.

THE URBAN
GUERRILLA

(courtesy W.M.)

Get into the cab before telling the driver your destination. Your chances are higher of getting to where you're going. If a cab driver is giving you a bum steer, tell him, "You're in violation of the law, Mr. Jones, hack number 374912," and he should get the message. No cabby wants to be reported. If this doesn't work say, "Okay. Take me to the nearest precinct."

If you're a visitor to the city, ask the concierge of your hotel how far your destination is and approximately what the fare should be before you board a taxi. That way you'll have an idea of what to expect. Another alternative is to ask for a reputable car service in the area.

Why complain you say? Besides, tomorrow night you're heading back to Peoria. If not for your complaint, your aunt Mildred might have the misfortune of getting the same bum cabby who takes her to the Bronx via the New Jersey Turnpike.

THE $30 FLAT AIRPORT FEE

In an effort to reduce overcharging the TLC has put into effect a $30 flat fee for passengers traveling from JFK Airport into Manhattan (not including tip and tolls). This measure is only *from* the airport, not *going to* because as the city agency stated, "passengers going to the airport usually hire cars in advance and seem to be more vulnerable coming into the city." Other boroughs are not included in the flat rate.

TAXI RIDER'S BILL OF RIGHTS

As a taxi rider you have the right to...

1. Direct the destination and route used.
2. A courteous English-speaking driver.
3. A driver who knows and obeys all traffic laws.
4. Air conditioning on demand.
5. Smoke and incense-free air.
6. A clean passenger and trunk area.

REFUSE TO TIP IF THE ABOVE ARE NOT COMPLIED WITH.

THE 10 WORST NEW YORK CAB DRIVERS
(Warning: If you find yourself in their taxi - escape FAST)

NAME	NUMBER OF VIOLATIONS	OFFENSE SPECIALTY
1. Sarbjeet Sahota	47	overcharging, speeding
2. Sung Min	43	abuse of passengers
3. Dial Singh	34	refusing service
4. Tarlochan Minhas	34	failing to cooperate
5. Manuel Criollo	33	failing to report accidents
6. Paul Christache	29	many traffic infractions
7. Ian McFarlane	25	arguing with passengers
8. Mohamed Zaman	23	overcharging passengers
9. Daniel Ojo	20	refusing service, fleecing
10. Raymond Colucci	19	overcharging, esp. preys on unsuspecting tourists

Source: Taxi & Limousine Commission

Taxi Cab Tricks of the Trade

By and large, most New York City cabbies are upstanding. However as in any profession, there are the good, the bad and the crummy. Some cabbies recently interviewed by Jon Hart of the *Manhattan Spirit* shared some of the scams they have used from time to time.

Rip-offs include the ***Shortchange Scam*** where a passenger is given the incorrect amount of change. For instance, a rider hands over a $20 bill for a $4 fare. The driver returns just 11 or 12 singles, hoping the customer won't even bother counting.

As mentioned earlier, some cabbies have gone to the trouble of installing ***Smaller Tires*** on their cabs so it will take more rotations and meter clicking to get to where you want to go. Others sometimes make it a practice of looking for a drunk to pick up -- a.k.a. ***Drunk Rolling.*** Once some intoxicated individual climbs aboard, the cabbie takes their wallet or possessions and dumps the drunk.

Probably the most popular scam especially among tourists is taking someone ***The Roundabout Way.*** This works when the cabbie takes a deliberately indirect route to your destination. Use a map beforehand and be able to specify the route your cabbie must follow.

Meter Rigging occurs when the fare box has been tampered with, causing it to jump more often. Unfortunately, it still is in practice about 25% of the time.

We've all been familiar with the ploy that starts out with your cabbie telling you that there's a bad traffic jam on such and such a route. Known as the ***Fake Traffic Jam Scam,*** passengers are then subject to taking a longer route to their destination.

HAILING A CAB AT RUSH HOUR

☛ Getting a cab at rush hour is never easy. But there are things you can do to better stack the odds in your favor. First, consider that one of the best places to find taxis are in front of hotels or luxury buildings.

☛ Travelers with their antennae up find some success by waiting on an uptown street when most folks are going downtown. At least that way you're more likely to get a cab that is heading back, looking for another fare.

☛ Of course if all else fails and you know you're going to be late, why not try sharing a ride? Yes, this is New York but stranger things have happened. All you have to do is ask. It saves both time and money.

NEW YORK FUN FACT

The Taxi and Limousine Commission reports that their office receives about 60 complaints against cab drivers daily. There are about 600,000 taxi trips made on any given day.

KEY NUMBERS

- *Taxi & Limousine Commission*   302-TAXI
  221 West 41st Street, New York, NY 10036

IF THE ABOVE HOTLINE PROVES TO BE COLD, CALL
- *TLC Commissioner's Office*   840-4520

Street enforcement is still maintained by the NYPD while the TLC inspectors deal primarily with livery and gypsy cabs.

In a effort to bring civility to the New York City cab driver, the TLC has worked in 50 new courteous sample sentences as part of their new cab driving training classes. Imagine hearing sentences such as these from your New York cabbie:

- "I'm sorry if you think I am driving too fast, sir/Madame. I will slow down immediately". *(But my meter works best when I'm doing 90)*

- "May I help you into the building Madame (sir)?" *(I need to use your toilet anyway)*

- "Madame (sir), would you care to listen to anything on the radio?" *(They're really rockin' on "Abdul's Request Line")*

- "I'm sorry, I made a wrong turn. I'll take care of it, and we can deduct it from the fare". *(Just don't forget to give me a bigger gratuity)*

- "It is my pleasure to place your bags in my trunk" *(Only don't expect to get them back anywhere in the near future)*

- "Madame (sir), is the temperature okay for you?" *(I can either blow on you or help get you excited)*

Get A Grip: John Kerschbaum says that if you tell your cabbie to go to hell beware -- you will be responsible for paying the tolls.

"HONEY. WE'VE JUST BEEN MUGGED"
16 STREETWISE TACTICS THAT REALLY WORK

New Yorker Ernest Castillo was walking to his mother's home one afternoon when off in the distance he heard a woman scream. As she turned the corner she appeared to be chasing someone. Several yards ahead of her was another woman trying to high tail it uphill with a handbag clenched in her fist.

Castillo was in a good position because both were running towards him on the opposite sidewalk He surveyed the scene carefully and thought he could outrun the mugger. He decided to go for it and took off after her. In his best police voice he shouted after her "Freeze!" The thief, caught by surprise, dropped the handbag. Castillo eventually caught up and threw her against a car. She fought back, shouted a few obscenities, and walked away defiantly. He made the decision not to pursue her since she had already surrendered the bag. Mr. Castillo didn't want to push his luck any further either....

The first woman, very attractive and out of breath, finally arrived to retrieve her bag. She thanked Castillo profusely. "Are you a cop"? she questioned. "No," he replied. "But I've always wanted to say *freeze* to someone -- just like in the movies." She thanked him again and smiled. He, still in his macho mode, walked away without ever getting her phone number. But he figured what the hell, at least I broke up a mugging and saved her purse. I also got to yell "freeze," -- just like in the movies.

As bad a rap as New Yorkers get for not coming to the aid of their neighbors, don't believe it for a moment. Today, more and more folks are getting involved.

New York was a city that until recently averaged 5 murders a day. Notice I said *was*. But with violent crime statistics dropping significantly (the city hasn't been this safe since 1970) it is still not a laughing matter to be mugged. After the fact, you'll feel embarrassed, humiliated, shocked and angry.

Take it from someone who has been there. While you're going through a rainbow of emotions, no matter how futile a gesture it may seem -- report the crime to the police. You have just 1 week to do this so that you may be eligible for compensation from the NYS Crime Victims Board. Additionally, your report may help the police track crimes, deploy their forces, and arrest more perpetrators. The precinct in the area needs to know what's going on in their very own backyard. Very possibly you'll be sparing the next innocent soul from going through what you've had to endure.

If your ability to work has been impaired as a result of a violent crime, the state can pay you a weekly salary for up to 26 weeks. Besides calling 911 and reporting the crime, give a description of the individual(s) and what was stolen. You should also call the Victims Services Hotline at 212-577-7777 which will help offer counseling and funds for such losses as broken locks, windows, etc.

Let's start with the concept that anyone at anytime can be a potential victim. Here are some facts that even a jaded New Yorker might not know.

☞ *Fact*: Muggers usually pick easy targets. Many of us don't want to work any harder than we already have to and muggers are no different. Ninety-nine out of a hundred times they look for the easy way and the path of least resistance.

☞ *Fact:* If you're easily distracted, look like you're lost in thought, especially by yourself, oblivious to what's going on around you -- or allow people on the street to stop you -- you will soon increase your chances dramatically for the position of "victim."

☞ *Fact:* Those doing the muggings actually prefer people who are not on the move. What's more, they do what they have to in order to get you to stop by either pretending to be lost, asking for a light, or perhaps asking for spare change.

☞ *Fact:* Street violence is a part of our lives on a daily basis across the entire country. For heaven's sake use common sense. Trust your pulse rate and the hair on the back of your neck.

16 SUPER STREETWISE TACTICS THAT HELP LOWER THE ODDS IN YOUR FAVOR

☞ Don't stop for someone who looks strange or suspicious or who asks you for a match. If you're more concerned with what the other person might think of you for passing them by -- you qualify for the title of potential victim.

☞ Be alert. Muggers look for people who are preoccupied and who aren't paying attention. Try not to use headphones when you walk down the street (especially at night) and don't tie up your hands.

☞ When you walk down the street, make sure you walk in the middle of the sidewalk or near the curb. That way you can see up ahead of you and around the corner. You'll also be able to avoid alleyways and doorways from which muggers can spring.

☞ During late hours especially, take the safe way to where you are headed even if it means walking a little out of your way.

☞ Walk with a purposeful stride. Above all be conscious of what's going on around you and up ahead. Don't be lost in thought or look like you don't know where you're going. Have your keys ready *before* you get to your apartment.

☞ Trust your instincts! They took thousands of years to develop. Many times that is all you have to go by. When the hair on the back of your neck stands up your instincts are warning you about some impending danger. When your heart races, listen to it.

☞ Don't ever buzz someone in your building unless you know who they are. Even if they say they lost their keys or are working in the building. Very often muggers press as many buttons as possible hoping someone will let them in.

☞ Stand clear of areas where groups of neighborhood youths hang out. Get on the other side of the street if you have to. Being street smart is avoiding trouble before it starts.

☞ Make occasional eye contact. Criminals don't want to be recognized.

☞ Don't count large amounts of cash in public or at the bank. Chances are you're being watched.

☞ Watch where you sit. Research indicates that you will be most vulnerable if you sit by an exit door, an open window or at a table at an outdoor cafe.

☞ Don't think that it can't happen to you because you're in a safe neighborhood. *Anyone* can become a victim at any given moment. Even if you think you know what you're doing.

☞ Men: Never keep your wallet or your money in your back pocket (aka *'suckcr pocket'*) since it is the most vulnerable to being picked. If you absolutely must keep it there put an unbreakable plastic comb in your wallet with the teeth pointed up. Put a large rubber band around the wallet. It will create a friction if someone tries to lift your wallet.

☛ If you do get mugged, get rid of the John Wayne/Jean-Claude Van Damm mentality and keep calm. Show that you are willing to cooperate. If you have a weapon pointed at you, tell the mugger where your wallet is. Your wallet or handbag is not worth risking your life over. Don't move suddenly. They're probably just as nervous as you. The key here is to cooperate.

☛ Women: If you think you're being followed: walk with your handbag upside down. Keep your hand on the clasp or zipper. If anybody does pull it, the contents of your bag will fall onto the sidewalk. The thief is not expected to stop and pick up the items.

☛ Don't hang your handbag on the back of your seat or on the floor of the restaurant. Avoid putting it on the empty seat next to you at the movie theater. If there are two of you walking down the street, keep it in between.

☛ Don't keep your keys in your handbag or with your car keys. Keep them separate. If your handbag or car is stolen, a thief will have access to your apartment. Above all look alert.

THE URBAN GUERRILLA

If you're walking home late at night, it's a good idea to invest in an emergency flare. You can purchase one at your nearest hardware or auto accessory store. Getting a whistle or mace out of your bag can be a very time-consuming chore. Having a flare ready to light up the sky with can prove to be quite spectacular. Extraordinary times call for extraordinary measures.

When walking down a deserted street, carry your unopened flare in your hand. When confronted by any suspicious stranger: pull the string, strike the flare and yell, "FIRE." Make no mistake about it -- your efforts will not go unnoticed.

NEW YORK FUN FACT

The New York City police car is a Chevrolet Caprice. A New York City *undercover* police car is an unmarked dark navy blue Caprice. Don't expect the driver to be wearing a uniform either.

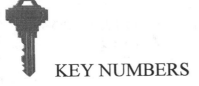

KEY NUMBERS

- Crime Victims Board of NYS   577-5160
270 Broadway (nr Chambers St.) 2nd Fl.
(financial aid and out of pocket medical expenses for victims
of crime)

- Crime Stoppers   577-8477
- Crime Victims Hotline   577-7777
- Special Victims Squad   694-3010
  (Sex crimes and child abuse)
- Rape Hotline   267-7273
- Guardian Angels Safety Patrol   397-7822
  763 Eighth Avenue

- Crime Prevention Division NYPD   718-776-6888
- Transit Police   718-330-3333

- To find out the closest precinct   374-5000

IF YOU ARE NOT GETTING SATISFACTION WITH YOUR LOCAL PRECINCT CALL...

- *New York City Police Commissioner's office* 374-5577

5 NEIGHBORHOODS WHERE YOU ARE MOST LIKELY TO GET ASSAULTED

	Number of assaults
• Central Harlem, Manhattan	1,076
• East Harlem, Manhattan	484
• Mott Haven, Hunts Pt., Bronx	482
• Highbridge, Morrisania, Bronx	627
• Chelsea, Manhattan	259

Source: NYC Health Dept.

HIGHEST NUMBER OF FELONY CRIMES BY PRECINCT

Bronx: The 44th and 46th precincts -- 7,635 felony crimes.

Brooklyn: 73,75,77,79,81,83,84,88,90 and 94th -- 25,558 felony crimes and 580 shootings.

Manhattan: 7th & 9th precincts -- 3,402 felony crimes.

Source: NYPD - 1995

NYC POLICE PRECINCTS

MANHATTAN

1st Precinct   16 Ericsson Place   334-0611
Patrol area: W Houston & south -- Bway to 12th Av

5th Precinct   19 Elizabeth Street   334-0711
area: East Houston and south -- Bway to Allen St.

6th Precinct   233 W. 10th St.   741-4811
area: West Houston to West 14th St.

7th Precinct   19 1/2 Pitt St.   477-7311
area: E Houston & South - Allen St. to East River

9th Precinct   321 E. 5th St.   477-7811
area: East Houston to East 14th St.

10th Precinct 230 W. 20th St.   741-8211
area: W 14th St. to W 43rd St.--12th Av to 7th Av

13th Precinct   230 East 21st St.   477-7411
area: E 14th St. to E 29th St. -- East River to 7th Ave

Midtown South 357 W. 35th St.   239-9811
area: 29th St. to 45th St. -- 9th Ave to Lexington Ave

17th Precinct   167 E. 51st St.   826-3211
area: E 29th St. to E 59th St. --   Lexington Ave to East
River

Midtown North 306 W. 54th St.   767-8400
area: W 43rd St. to W 59th St. - 12th Ave to Lex.
W 45-E 45 Sts

19th Precinct 153 E. 67th St. 452-0600
area: East 59th St. to East 96th St. -- 5th Ave to East River

20th Precinct 120 W. 82nd St. 580-6411
area: W 59th St. -- W 86th St. -- Central Park West to 12th Ave

Central Park 86th St. & Transverse Rd 570-4820
area: all of Central Park from 59th St. to Central Park North

23rd Precinct 164 E. 102nd St. 860-6411
area: E 96th St. to E 114th St. -- 5th Ave to East River

24th Precinct 151 W. 100th St. 678-1811
area: West 86th St. to Cathedral Pkwy - Central Park West to West Side Hwy.

25th Precinct 120 E. 199th St. 860-6511
area: East 115th St. to East 133rd St.

26th Precinct 520 W. 126th St. 678-1311
area: Cathedral Pkwy - W 133rd St - Morningside Av to West Side Hwy

28th Precinct 2271 8th Ave 678-1611
area: Central Park No. - W 127th St - 5th Ave to Morningside Ave

30th Precinct 451 W. 151st St. 690-8811
area: W 133rd St. - W 155th St. - Edgecomb Av to West Side Hwy

32nd Precinct 250 W. 135th St. 690-6311
area: W 127th St. - W 155th St. - 5th Ave to Edgecomb Av

34th Precinct   4295 Broadway   927-9711
area: W 155th St. to Northern end of Manhattan

BRONX

40 Precinct	257 Alexander Ave	718	402-2270
41 Precinct	1035 Longwood Ave	718	542-4771
42 Precinct	830 Washington Ave	718	402-3887
43 Precinct	900 Fteley Ave	718	542-0888
44 Precinct	2 East 169th St	718	590-5511
45 Precinct	2877 Barkley Ave	718	822-5411
46 Precinct	2120 Ryer Ave	718	220-5211
47 Precinct	4111 Laconia Ave	718	920-1211
48 Precinct	450 Cross Bronx Exp.	718	299-3900
49 Precinct	2121 Eastchester Rd	718	918-2000
50 Precinct	3450 Kingsbridge Ave	718	543-5700
52 Precinct	3016 Webster Ave	718	220-5811

BROOKLYN

60 Precinct	2951 West 8th St	718	946-3311
61 Precinct	2575 Coney Island Ave	718	627-6611
62 Precinct	1925 Bath Ave	718	236-2611
63 Precinct	1844 Brooklyn Ave	718	258-4411
66 Precinct	5822 16th Ave	718	851-5611
67 Precinct	2820 Snyder Ave	718	287-3211
68 Precinct	333 65th St	718	439-4211
69 Precinct	9720 Foster Ave	718	257-6211
70 Precinct	154 Lawrence Ave	718	851-5511
71 Precinct	421 Empire Blvd	718	735-0511
72 Precinct	830 4th Ave	718	965-6311
73 Precinct	1470 East N.Y. Ave	718	495-5411
75 Precinct	1000 Sutter Ave	718	827-3511
76 Precinct	191 Union St	718	834-3211
77 Precinct	127 Utica Ave	718	735-0611
78 Precinct	65 6th Ave	718	636-6411

79 Precinct	263 Tompkins Ave	718	636-6611
81 Precinct	30 Ralph Ave	718	574-0411
83 Precinct	480 Knickerbocker	718	574-1605
84 Precinct	301 Gold St	718	875-6811
88 Precinct	298 Classon Ave	718	636-6511
90 Precinct	211 Union Ave	718	963-5311
94 Precinct	100 Meserole Ave	718	383-3879

QUEENS

100 Precinct	92-24 Rockaway Bch	718	318-4200
101 Precinct	16-12 Mott Ave	718	868-3400
102 Precinct	87-34 118th Ave	718	805-3200
103 Precinct	168-02 91st Ave	718	657-8181
104 Precinct	64-02 Catalpa Ave	718	386-3004
105 Precinct	92-08 222nd St	718	776-9090
106 Precinct	103-51 101st St	718	845-2211
107 Precinct	71-01 Parsons Blvd	718	969-5100
108 Precinct	5-47 50th Ave	718	784-5411
109 Precinct	37-05 Union St	718	321-2250
110 Precinct	91-41 43rd Ave	718	476-9311
111 Precinct	45-06 215th St	718	279-5200
112 Precinct	68-40 Austin St	718	520-9311
113 Precinct	167-02 Baisley Blvd	718	712-7733
114 Precinct	34-16 Astoria Blvd	718	626-9311
115 Precinct	92-15 Northern Blvd	718	533-2002

STATEN ISLAND

120 Precinct	78 Richmond Terr	718	876-8500
122 Precinct	2320 Hylan Blvd	718	667-2211
123 Precinct	116 Main St	718	948-9311

#5

IT CAME FROM OUT OF THE BLUE :
KETCHUP CHUCKING
(& OTHER BIG CITY SCAMS)

"I was making a deposit at my bank in a neighborhood that I wasn't really familiar with," said David L. a native of Flushing. "I needed to cash a check and then I had a few minutes to kill."

David, an outside sales representative whose work takes him to different parts of the city, considers himself street savvy. But on that hot summer day several years ago, he was not aware that he was being watched very carefully by three individuals who had selected him as their next "mark." He fit the criteria to a tee. "Looking back I guess I made some mistakes," said the New Yorker. "I looked like I didn't know where I was going. I was wearing my good suit and I was arrogant enough to believe that this sort of thing doesn't happen to a native New Yorker."

After cashing his check, he left the bank and proceeded to walk down lower Broadway at a rather leisurely pace. "Next thing I know I'm being splattered from the back with this sticky syrup.

When I turned around there were three soft spoken, middle aged people shocked at what had happened to me." Soon afterwards the female in the group helped try to get the stain off his jacket while the others watched. "They told me it came from an office window up above and one took out a handful of Kleenex." Next thing he knew his cash was suddenly gone along with the three 'good Samaritans' who disappeared into a nearby car. It sped off into traffic and was never seen again.

What David was exposed to is known as *Ketchup Chucking,* a street scam described by Detective Angel Ortiz, from the Special Frauds division of NYPD as "affecting creatures of habit who follow the same routine." It occurs when people aren't alert," said Ortiz. Whatsmore it's not only the elderly who are targets. *Ketchup Chucking* begins when one inadvertently makes the mistake of displaying a large amount of money or merchandise in public.

Perhaps you're counting your cash at the teller's window or paying a bill. Your transaction is an open book to the inconspicuous onlooker. Everything from here on will appear as an accident. Suddenly without warning you feel something hit your clothes. It comes from when you least expect it.

Maybe it came from the guy eating a weenie. Perhaps it was the lady slurping her Hagen Daaz low fat yogurt. Everything looks innocent enough. The parties involved appear reputable, well dressed, even try to help undo the damage.

The more and more these folks try to help you, the more your faith in mankind has been restored. But something's wrong, these strangers are rubbing and wiping your clothes as though their lives depend on it. You don't feel a thing. The idea was to distract you, a.k.a. *misdirection,* a practice used by sleight-of-hand specialists.

"Ketchup chucking" works when one accomplice distracts you while their accomplice lifts your money. "First thing is, you really can't trust anybody you don't know on the street" Ortiz explained. "A lot of the teams operating will first approach you for help. Be alert. Take a step back and hold onto your property."

The detective continued by saying, "The way you become vulnerable is by being surrounded and misdirected while an accomplice picks your pocket."

GET A GRIP

- One is usually not in danger of *Ketchup Chucking* unless one makes an open display of cash or expensive packages in public. To begin with, con artists want to qualify a victim as being worth their while. After all, time *is* money.

- Remember, cons have practiced this maneuver consistently and professionally with all the skill of fine craftsmen. You are no match for them. However take consolation, there *are* ways you can foil their schemes.

If you do find yourself in the midst of condiment-smearing and someone tries to help you by taking a sudden interest in your clothes -- hold onto your property and yell for the police. Don't be afraid to make a scene. Con men don't want attention..

- Don't be preoccupied and in a daze. If you do go to a branch of your bank in a neighborhood you're not familiar with, be observant of what's going on around you.

- If you do get hit with some foreign substance, *don't have anybody help you. THE STAIN IS THERE SO LEAVE IT!*

- Take a step back and say, "Thank you very much but I can do this on my own" and *WALK AWAY! EVEN IF IT KILLS YOU WALK AWAY AS FAST AS YOU CAN!*

Something about your demeanor drew these parasites to you. Above all remember, if you stand there for any length of time with someone who does take an active interest, rest assured that you will get ripped off 99 out of 100 times. Granted, there are some nice folks out there who might offer to help. But there is no way for you to know who is who. It is in your best interests to leave the scene immediately. If you are still being followed, duck into a nearby store or restaurant and call 911. Then you can have your clothes scotchguarded like the rest of us.

THE GUM BALL MACHINE

Next time you see a gumball machine that promises to split the profits with a charity think twice about dropping your quarter in the slot. Most charities only get 2 cents out of a quarter and that boils down to less than 10 percent. In some cases the vendor pockets 95% of the donation.

Typically, a charity allows a vendor to use it's name in exchange for 5 or 10 per cent of the gross according to the National Charities Foundation. Many charities believe vendors are taking in far more money than they indicate on their balance sheets. If you want to buy some gum then buy it across the counter and write a check to a charity. At least that way you'll be certain where the money went.

CHOCOLATE BAR SCAM

You've seen some kids wearing forlorn expressions on their faces while they hawk Nestle Crunch Bars on the streets of the city. They claim that if you just buy a candy bar that the proceeds will go to either their school, church or youth center. So what would normally cost you 65 cents now sells for the outrageous price of $2.00 or three bucks if you buy two. But can you be sure whose pocket the donation winds up in? It's probably a gift to the kid, not the charity. When you give cash there is usually a lack of accountability. National Charities Foundation says, "when in doubt -- don't give."

If you have any question as to the nature or legitimacy of the 'charity,' one way of finding out for sure is by calling the New York office of the National Charities Information Bureau at 929-6300. You may also request a free copy of the organization's *Wise Giving Guide* which evaluates 300 charities by writing to: National Charities Information Bureau, Dept. 502, 19 University Square West, New York, NY 10003.

TELEPHONE SLAMMING

The illegal practice of switching your long distance carrier without your permission is all too familiar to many. The reality is that you won't know about it until after you receive a more costly phone bill. Be warned that some companies will even use a phony sweepstakes entry that you fill out as authorization for such a move.

Get A Grip: Dial 00 to verify your long distance carrier. Next, instruct your phone company to freeze your long distance carrier. That way only you can change it by written request. Report the slammers to the PSC 800-342-3377.

NEW INTERNET FRAUD

The National Consumers League, a nonprofit organization reports that internet fraud is on the rise. Scams to be wary of include pyramid schemes, bogus internet-related services, phony equipment sellers, fraudulent business opportunities and work-at-home offers. The Internet Fraud Watch which monitors scams can be reached at (800) 876-7060 or at their web site at http:///www.fraud.org.

SWINDLING SINGLES

While most introduction and dating services are honest, there are others to be wary of. To begin with, the legal limit membership to any of these organizations is a 1,000 contract-fee. If anybody asks you for more, it's a sure indication that you shouldn't be doing business with them. Watch out for extra fees for additional services.

Get A Grip: Don't be afraid to ask lots of questions, talk to previous customers and call The Better Business Bureau (Pg. 30) to see what kind of rating they have.

NO BUSINESS LIKE SHOW BIZ SCAM

Watch out for so-called 'agents' or 'personal managers' who will charge you a fee to work with them. It's a sure sign that they are not legit. You should not be required to pay for test shots by a prospective representation. Modeling agencies are required to be licensed by the Department of Consumer Affairs.

More than half of all complaints received by the DCA are for modeling agencies.

Get a Grip: If you have any doubt whatsoever about it, call the Screen Actors Guild (212-944-1030) to see if the agency is registered. Standard commissions with legitimate agents and managers range from 10-15%.

HOME IMPROVEMENT

Always check out several contractors and get written estimates that include the cost of materials, description of work and the completion time. Go to previous customers to see if they're satisfied. Home improvement contractors are among the top ten most complained about businesses so use extra caution before you're ready to sign your life away. Many scams take place immediately after a fire or flood.

Get A Grip: Check with the Department of Consumer Affairs to see if the business is licensed. Insist on a written contract and only give one third deposit at the signing of the contract. A third when the job is half done and a third when the job is completed.

NEW YORK FUN FACT

Street scams and rip-offs fall into the category of Larceny. From Jan-April 1995 - 20,434 grand larceny cases were reported city wide of which there were only 2,817 arrests.

1,575 of the cases were cleared.

Source: NYPD

KEY NUMBERS

- *Police Headquarters*   374-6850
  Special Fraud Division
  One Police Plaza

- *Elderly Crime Victims Resource Ctr.*   442-3103
  280 Broadway, New York, NY 10007

- *New York State Attorney General*   416--8345
  General Consumer Complaint Division

- *National Fraud Information Center*   800-876-7060

#6

WHAT YOU DIDN'T KNOW ABOUT 3 CARD MONTE

3 Card Monte has been referred to by one New Yorker as "the longest running show on Broadway." If you're either a resident or visitor of this city you've probably seen or heard about this street hustle. It's played in heavy pedestrian traffic with a stack of cardboard boxes, three slightly bent playing cards, and perpetrated by what seems to be a poor person.

This ploy enables teams of con artists to make several hundred dollars a day separating you from your wallet in a matter of minutes. *Even* if you think it can't happen to you.

3 Card Monte is one of the oldest con games around, dating back to the War of 1812 and only surpassed in age by *The Shell Game*. Folks back then got taken for being suckers in much the same way they do today. Some things never change.

To start with, *3 Card Monte* is played on a busy street with the hope of attracting a crowd. The dealer of the game, usually a fast talker, dares any onlooker to find the red card out of three -- the other 2 cards are black. At first all he wants you to do is point to the red card (innocent enough). Then he *even* lets you hold his money as an act of good faith. What a guy! (There are some very skillful women dealers around too.)

The last and most important step is for you to make a small friendly wager of a mere twenty bucks. "You're asked to chose one card and they're paying even money so the odds are automatically wrong" says long time magician and Vice President of the Tannen Magic Store in New York, John Blake. "It should be 2 to 1."

Granted, all of this to the lay person looks like an easy way to score a fortune (for the dealer *not for you*). There are always those who are convinced that they can win. Yet the sad reality to *3 Card Monte* is more and more innocent souls fall prey to this rip-off each and every year by losing their hard-earned vacation money. It all begins with greed.

Here's the way it works. The operation usually consists of 5 individuals. One dealer, two shills (one possibly female) and two lookouts. The shill's sole function is to blend in with the crowd. Shills appear to bet aggressively and to be winning. A less-than-obvious shill might encourage an onlooker to bet on what appears to be a sure thing. Some might tell you the game isn't on the level just to gain your confidence. Many times the team is made up of mixed races. There is also a disparity in the way the dealer and shill dress to avoid association.

Keep in mind that while all this is going on, there are two lookouts on the team (not easily spotted), making sure that the cops aren't within striking distance. If they do see the cops, they shout a password, the dealer and the shills walk away from the operation (usually in different directions), and they wait until the coast is clear before resuming the scam.

Penn Jillette of the illusionist-comedy team, *Penn & Teller*, made a public service message that aired on New York TV stations several years ago. There he warned tourists never to play the game under any circumstances. The spot was even translated into Japanese.

"No matter how smart you are, how lucky you are, you will lose! If you think it's some poor person on the street with just a cardboard box and you can take their money, you're going to be wrong," warned Jillette. At any given hour in Times Square people are still convinced they can win.

When the dealer appears to be tossing the bottom card, he can maneuver and throw any card. This one maneuver is virtually impossible to follow. "It's not a matter of how fast the dealer is. It's switching and misdirecting your attention just for a brief moment," says Blake. While it's possible to pick the right card, the idea is that the team never lets you win. In this scenario, the dealer will then insist on a higher bet. When the victim hesitates, one of the shills will put up the money and collect.

Another technique used when the winning card is picked, is for the shill to yell: "Cops." Suddenly the game breaks up. Whatever the situation, the idea is to not let anyone win even once. If they do, chances are it's a shill.

There have been as many as 100 or more *Three Card Monte* and Shell game operators at any given time in New York City. Every year there is a move to crackdown on these pervasive and resilient teams, but all they seem to draw are 30 days in jail if we're lucky. In some cases they're back out on the streets the very next day. Being arrested is not necessarily a deterrent. Very often the dealers have learned their trade in prison.

GET A GRIP

- Even if by some small miracle you *think* you've won something, you can rest assured that you'll be relieved of that feeling and your assets very quickly. Members of the operation will help empty your pockets once you have taken some additional steps and turn the corner.
  "This is their business. They're not going to let you walk away with their money," says Blake.

- Of course I realize that even with this warning to stay clear of the scam there'll be those idiots who will need to find out for themselves. Unfortunately, the scenario that follows is always the same. Some poor soul winds up betting more in a futile effort to get back the first batch of cash he lost. The result is he winds up losing his trousers and his "I love NY" T-shirt.

- Why don't the police help? According to article #225 of the New York penal law, People Vs. William's 1978, the state legislature ruled that *Three Card Monte* is considered gambling <u>not</u> fraud because the victim <u>voluntarily</u> agrees to play along. Those who take part in this con game have a slim to zero chance of recovering their money. The victim in this game is a person who thinks they can get something for nothing.

Another variation of Monte is *The Shell Game.* It is played with a tiny red ball of wax that's placed under a bottle cap. It's the same rip-off. You can stop and watch but *keep your cash where it is.*

As John Blake was quick to point out, "If people are that interested in gambling they should go to a casino."

NEW YORK FUN FACT

A bill is being introduced (Intro. 527) to the city council by Councilmember Andrew Eristoff to outlaw *Three Card Monte* from the streets of New York City. This despite the fact that NYS Criminal Court (the *honorable* Sheryl L. Parker) ruled that Monte is a game of skill and exempt from state gambling laws. Way to go Sheryl!

If you're observing *Three Card Monte* from a distance and the dealer asks you just to show 20 or 40 dollars, or if they assure you it's just for fun, don't do it! No matter how innocent a gesture it may seem -- this is just another ploy to take the money out of your hand so that it looks like you wagered a bet. It will be next to impossible to get it back.

KEY NUMBER

- *Gamblers Anonymous*   *265-8600*

#7

STICKING IT TO THE PICKPOCKETS

Keep your eye on your wallets gang. Pickpockets have gotten more sophisticated and work in very structured teams. If you give these parasites the opportunity -- it is for sure they will seize the moment, this according to new larceny unit of the Police Department which tracks down the culprits.

The teams have one member for every function of the operation. The person who picks the victim is the 'steerer', while the pickpocket is the 'dip'. Close by is the 'stall' who distracts or slows down the victim and the 'dish' who takes the wallet from the dip. In the midst is the 'shield' who blocks the view and lastly the 'tailpipe' who remains the lookout.

Worst Pickpocket Zones to Watch Out For:

💣 Port Authority (40-42 Sts. 8th-9th Aves.)
💣 Rockefeller Center-Radio City Music Hall area
💣 Theater District
💣 Bloomingdale's area,
💣 Grand Central Station
💣 Penn Station

Worst Subway Stations for being pickpocketed

💣 59th Street-Third Ave
💣 51st Street-Lexington Ave
💣 50th Street-Broadway

GET A GRIP

HOW TO MAKE A PICKPOCKET HAVE THE KIND OF DAY YOU'RE HAVING

• If you know that you've just had your pocket picked, scream and make a commotion. Call out and warn the driver or conductor. Alert everyone that there's a pickpocket on board. Don't be afraid to shout.

• Beware of loud arguments or commotions. Incidents can be staged to distract you while your pocket is picked.

- Pickpockets work in teams. Their favorite spots are anywhere people congregate, especially escalators and crowded streets. Avoid crowding in the area of subway doors. In restaurants -- don't sit near the door or exits.

- Carrying any kind of bag *without* a closed zipper, flap or clasp is asking for trouble. Keep your bag zippered shut and slung crosswise over your shoulders.

- Men never walk around with money in your back pants pocket. It is the easiest to pick.

- Keep your money in your shirt pocket right under your nose. It is the hardest pocket to pick.

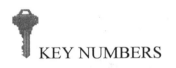

KEY NUMBERS

- *Crime Victims Hotline*   577-7777

- *Closest Police Precinct to you*   374-5000

- *Crime Stoppers*   577-8477

THE URBAN GUERRILLA

Watch out for those who appear to stumble in front of you on public transportation while exiting or when someone seems to have dropped something in the stairwell of a bus. Be aware of any pushing or shoving near the exit doors.

The most likely target continues to be one who is oblivious to what's going on around them and those who think it can't happen to them.

#7

WHAT IN THE WORLD
DID YOU JUST EAT?

According to government nutrition guidelines, one's daily food intake should not exceed 65 grams of fat, 2,000 calories, 2400 Mgs of sodium and 20 grams of saturated fat. Nutritionists say only 30% of your calories should come from fat.

Consumer advocate David Horowitz recommends taking *The Fat Test.* If a product (like a bagel, roll, etc.,) claims to be fat free, place it in a brown paper bag and wait and see after an hour if there are any oil stains on the bag. If there are, what you are about to eat is not fat free.

FAST FOOD FAT CONTENT

MCDONALDS

Sausage Biscuit with egg	35g
Arch Deluxe	31g
with bacon	34g
Triple Cheeseburger	30g
Quarter Pounder with cheese	29g
McChicken Sandwich	29g

TACO BELL

Taco Salad	55g
Chicken Burritto Supreme	23g
7 Layer Burritto	23g
BLT Double Decker Taco	20g

BURGER KING

Double Whopper w/cheese	63g
Double Whopper Sandwich	56g
Chicken Sandwich	43g
BK Big Fish Sandwich	43g
Croissan'wich with sausage, egg/cheese	41g
Double cheeseburger w/bacon	39g

ROY ROGERS

Big Country Platter w/sausage	60g
Sourdough Bacon Cheeseburger	50g
Big Country Platter w/bacon	43g
" " " w/ham	39g

9 piece Nuggets	29g
1/4 Cheeseburger	26g
Chicken Fillet	24g

WENDY'S

Big Bacon Classic	36g
Taco Salad	30g
Chicken Club Sandwich	25g
Jr. Bacon Cheeseburger	25g

KENTUCKY FRIED CHICKEN

Chicken Pot Pie	40g
Hot and Spicy chicken breast	35g
Hot Wings - 6 pieces	33g
Extra Tasty Crispy breast	28g
Colonel's Chicken Sandwich	27g
Original Recipe breast	20g
Potato Salad	17g

PIZZA HUT

Pepperoni personal pan pizza	29g
Pepperoni pan pizza	25g
Sausage pan pizza	24g
Meat lover's pan pizza	23g

DUNKIN DONUTS

Chocolate croissant	29g
Almond croissant	27g
Glazed chocolate ring	21g
Plain croissant	19g
Glazed whole wheat ring	18g
Plain cake ring	17g

Glazed buttermilk ring   14g

KIDS MEALS

Burger King	32g
Arbys	27g
Wendys	26g
MacDonalds	24g
Kentucky Fried Chicken *(least amount of food)*	17g

THE 8 WORST FOODS IN *SATURATED* FAT

Highest levels of saturated fat are found in products from animals sources, i.e. meats, eggs, cheese. This is the type of artery clogging fat most of us are concerned with. Unsaturated fat comes from plant sources, i.e., oats, corn, etc. The only saturated fats that come from plants are palm and coconut oils. Even raw vegetables have some measure of saturated fat in them but have no cholesterol.

Roy Rogers Chicken Fillet	24g
Contadina Alfredo Sauce	21g
Libby's Corned Beef Hash	17g
Just 2 hot dogs	14g
Swanson Chicken Pot Pie	14g
Ben & Jerry's Ice Cream	14g
Oscar Mayer Lunchables	13g
Hostess's Ho Ho's	12g

HEALTHY ALTERNATIVES

- Vegetables
- Fruits
- Meats (that you can select, trim and cook)

Other Foods that are Low in Fat

- Gravy
- Parmesean cheese
- Soups

Acceptable levels of saturated fat should consist of
20 grams a day for women
28 grams a day for men

Note: Saturated fat should only be about 10% of your caloric intake

WATCH OUT FOR WHAT'S LURKING IN THAT BURGER!

The Food and Drug Administration reports
that the E-Coli bacteria has reached
epidemic status in the U.S. and is mostly
found in hamburger meat. This bacteria is
found in the intestines and feces of cows and sometimes gets
passed onto the meat that humans consume. E-Coli bacteria
was first discovered in 1982 and at last estimates, 20,000
cases are reported yearly with 500 fatalities.

Get-A-Grip: The E-Coli bacteria cannot survive above a
temperature of 155°. Don't order your burger rare, medium

rare or medium well. Order it well done or don't order it at all! If the inside of your hamburger is pink or any red juices flow from it, don't eat it!

TOFU ALERT: When at the salad bar watch out for tofu that is left out in the open. Recent investigations report that left unprotected and in open water, it is filled with high counts of bacteria. Refrigeration below 40 degrees Fahrenheit kills bacteria. Experts recommend purchasing this product only when it's antiseptically packaged or when you can steam your tofu thoroughly.

HOLD THOSE CHOPSTICKS...

SUSHI - THE RAW FACTS

Before you bite into your next order of raw fish remember that raw foods are essentially safe havens for all kinds of bacteria. Contaminated sushi can cause tape worm, round worm, parasites, food poisoning, and cold sweats.

Nutritionist Dr. Joan Forbeack states that you can be sick and not know it. You may suddenly have flu like symptoms and in reality have a mild case of food poisoning. Every year there are about 33 million cases of food poisoning in this country.

Some believe that one should check and see if a restaurant's sushi chef has credentials in the fine art of sushi. Only the freshest fish, prepared with skill and carefully served, should become sushi. Whatever you do, it is recommended that you don't try to make these dishes at home.

SALAD BARS

Most folks don't know what they're shoveling into their bodies from their local eateries. Most often we never get to see the food handlers in the establishment and what they've done with their hands just prior to preparing food.

Salad bars are safe havens for high counts of bacteria. However, bacteria don't like to grow in an acidic (vinegary) environment.

ICED TEA

Large amounts of bacteria have shown up in ice tea among leading NY establishments. Some of the samples taken from Nathans, Burke & Burke, Starbucks, TGIF, and Houlihans and tested by microbiologists at Rutgers University show very high counts of coliforms, a type of bacteria which can induce food poisoning.

Unclean equipment, hands and incorrect brewing and storage are to blame. So avoid the ice tea whenever you can.

WORST TEA TO MAKE FOR YOURSELF

Sun Tea is probably the worst tea you can make for yourself. To make it you let tea bags steep in water and let the rays of the sun do the work. Lack of boiling invites bacteria into the process.

KEY NUMBER

- *NY Health Dept.*   442-9666
  (Food complaints in bars and restaurants)

IF THIS HOTLINE PROVES TO BE COLD - CALL

- *Special Assistant to the Commissioner*   788-5257

#9

BATTLE OF THE BOWL
ALWAYS AVAILABLE REST ROOMS
FOR WHEN DUTY CALLS

   Visitor and native New Yorker alike face the same difficulty in this city -- when you gotta go, the going gets tough. If you've spent any amount of time here, you'll concede that finding an available bathroom is no easy task. Signs that read, "Rest Rooms for Customers Only" bring little relief. Wolfing down a turkey burger or prune danish just to use the facility is akin to extortion.

The problem stems from the fact that New York City doesn't house public toilets, the one exception being the prototype pay toilet in City Hall Park behind the mayor's office, and that costs 25 cents a shot.

On the other hand if you walk into an establishment and are not wearing a skinny chicken on your head, more often than not, the management will let you use the facility. Studies reveal that women have an edge over men on gaining permission to use the commode. Maybe that's because most managers of restaurants tend to be lecherous males.

I recommend doing with rest rooms what Steven Spielberg did with Hollywood studios. When he had aspirations of being a director, he'd walk into a Hollywood lot with an air of certainty, as though he knew exactly where he was going. This technique, not only used for rest rooms, creates the impression that you belong.

For those of us in transit, particularly in cars, when the urge strikes, things become a bit more challenging. Just ask a cab driver what he does. The pee technique used by cabbies who have to go in a hurry and can't find a place to whiz consists of standing at the front of where their car door opens, unzipping and pretending that they're looking at something far away.

Devices for motorists who have to go in a hurry include a portable urinal called 'Little John' for men and a new device for women simply called *Le Funnel.* Either item can be used along roadsides and on hiking trails.

Just in case you find yourself stranded on Manhattan island and have had that one extra bowl of chili at the street fair -- here is a list of facilities that are usually available. Happy hunting!

GET A GRIP ...For when the going gets tough...

(Available rest rooms in New York City)

DOWNTOWN (below 14th Street)

New York University Loeb Student Center 566 LaGuardia at W 4th St. (opp. Wash. Sq. Park)	downstairs base of stair
City Hall between Broadway & Park Row	2nd floor
Surrogate Court Bldg. 31 Chambers St. (nr Centre St.)	men's 4th fl ladies 3rd fl
The New School 66 West 12th Street bet. 6th & 7th Aves	ground & 3rd floors
The Film Forum 209 W. Houston St. (Varick St. & 6th Ave)	to the left of box office no ticket or popcorn nec.

MIDTOWN (14th through 57th St.)

Barnes & Noble Bookstore West 21st St. & 6th Avenue	main floor rear

Penn Station
7th & 8th Avenues
bet 31-33rd Sts

near 8th Avenue escalator
entrance opp. track 17.

Manhattan Mall
33rd St. - Ave of Americas

floors 5 & 7

Grand Central Station
(Park & Lexington Aves)

ground fl. 42nd St.

...*You can skip this one by going just next door at the* Grand Hyatt Hotel - Main floor (A good deal more pleasant.)

The New York Public Library
Fifth Avenue branch
bet. 40-42nd Sts

3rd floor

Mid-Manhattan Public Library
40th Street & Fifth Avenue

3rd & 4th floors

Milford Plaza
44th Street & Eighth Aves

lobby - press # 31 on
combination lock

McDonalds
46th Street & Broadway

men's - rear of restaurant
ladies - 2nd floor

Waldorf Astoria
Park Avenue
bet 49-50th Sts

take stairs or escalator
up to lounge

GE Bldg.
30 Rockefeller Plaza
bet. 49-50th Sts

lower level near steps
to subway

Museum of Modern Art
11 West 53rd Street
bet 5th-6th Aves   all floors

Dept. Of Labor   go through double glass doors,
247 West 54th St.   main fl. ask guard for key
betw. 8th & Bway

The New York Hilton   2nd and 3rd floors
55th Street & 6th Ave   off up escalator to left

Trump Tower
5th Avenue
betw. 56-57th Sts   go to lower level by escalator

Sony Plaza
550 Madison av.   Through arcade into Sony Wonder
bet. 55-56th Sts   exhibit - main level

UPTOWN (59th Street and up)

Bloomingdale's   men's room in basement and
Lexington Ave, betw 59-60th Sts   on floors 5 & 7
                              ladies room 4 & 7

Avery Fisher Hall   Ground floor opp. restaurant
65th St. & Amsterdam Ave

Lincoln Center Library   on all three floors
111 Amsterdam Ave 65th St.   except main floor

Museum of Natural History
West 77-79th Sts   all floors except 4th

CENTRAL PARK REST ROOMS

(These are the closest thing we have to public rest rooms. Central Park has 19 rest rooms in all. Complaints about any of these facilities can be made directly to 800-201-7275.)

Wollman Skating Rink	63d St. - middle park
Sailboat Lake	74thSt. - Fifth Ave
Loeb Boat House	75th St. - middle park
Sheep's Meadow	67th St. - middle park
Tavern on the Green	67th St. - CPW
Delacorte Theater	81st St. - middle park
Conservatory Gardens	105th St. - Fifth Ave

BRYANT PARK

Betw. 40 & 42 Sts - 6th Ave   - middle of the park

THE URBAN GUERRILLA

Thanks to Alan Abel for this suggestion which requires a bit of chutzpah. When you enter a restaurant and are stopped by management, tell them you are the local health inspector of the neighborhood committee and you've come to inspect their toilet. If you're questioned about the organization you represent (which rarely happens), tell them it's a newly formed grass roots organization.

NEW YORK FUN FACT

Go in Style. How about at world famous Tavern on the Green? Rumor has it with local government that because this posh restaurant is located in Central Park, it's required to make its rest rooms available to the public. Then again it's not written in porcelain.

KEY NUMBERS

- *Parks Dept.*   800-201-7275
  (Complaints about Park Restrooms)

IF THIS HOTLINE PROVES TO BE COLD CALL;

- *Parks Dept. Commissioner's office*   360-1307

#10

WARNING

NOT ALL PAY TELEPHONES ARE ALIKE !
WHERE TO FIND ONE THAT WORKS

Spend any time in New York these days and you're bound to notice a difference in pay phones. A good many of them refuse to provide a dial tone let alone refund your quarter. In a world that is fast changing, be warned, not all pay phones in this city -- or the country for that matter -- are alike!

According to the New York Public Service Commission, the municipal agency that oversees such operations, more and more private pay phones are popping up all across the nation. "Currently there are about 50,000 of these privately-owned pay phones just in New York State," says Edward Collins, a spokesman for the Public Service Commission.

Approximately 18,000 of these phones are in New York City. They may *look* like the real thing but that's where the similarity ends.   These operations known as COCOT(s), *Customer Owned Currency Operated Telephones,* can be found anywhere.

In many cases, the owner of one such phone might very well be the establishment that houses the phone. The owner, for obvious reasons, prefers to keep a low profile by avoiding any problems concerning rates and refunds.

COCOTs first started appearing as early as 1985. "These operations don't have to be listed with any state or federal agency due to deregulation laws. But there are rules they still have to follow. We know the companies that operate them. The Federal Communications Commission has no jurisdiction over local calls[1]." Collins warned.

In some cases, there is also a fee for dialing directory assistance and in some cases you're even charged for "ringing time." Usually there's an out-of-state operator who in all likelihood doesn't have the authority to refund your money. Be prepared. You probably won't be asked for just five cents when it comes to an additional five minutes.

If you do lose money or dispute the charges in one of these pay phones, it generally is more difficult to retrieve. A good many hotels, restaurants, and other businesses are safe havens for COCOTS or OSP (Operator Service Providers) which charge 3-10 times more for long distance calls as compared to MCI, AT&T and Sprint. Use your own calling

---

[1] COCOT rates are very often higher than Nynex's (New York Telephone) so don't be ready to give out your credit card number, especially over a mobile phone since others can pick up your frequency.

card to be safe and try to avoid telephone companies you're
not familiar with.

GET A GRIP

- If you're using a Nynex phone, it will say so on the front
  of the unit. If you lose your money, just dial 211 and ask
  for credit. You will either have your home phone
  credited or receive a check for the difference.

- If it's a COCOT phone, life gets a little more
  complicated. First, dial the company. If there is no
  phone number on the unit, just dial 958; you'll find out
  the number with your quarter refunded.

- If you feel you've just been ripped off and are getting
  nowhere fast, call the PSC. The New York State Public
  Service Commission's toll free helpline, 800-342-3377,
  be prepared to wait and do it at your leisure. Tell them
  exactly where the phone is located, and be as specific as
  possible (*i.e. date and time of when you made the call,
  name of the company listed on the front of the phone*).

- If you're placing a call outside of the immediate vicinity,
  make sure you know the rates *before* you give out your
  credit or calling card number. Recent surveys indicate
  COCOT rates are always much higher than local
  providers.

- If the pay phone you're using is unregistered and ripping
  you off, call the Department of Information, Technology
  and Telecommunications (718-243-2500). The way to
  find out if a pay phone is registered is to look on the front
  of it for "owned and operated by:" If there is no

> information in this space -- it is probably unregistered and illegal.

NEW PSC WEB SITE

You may also file a complaint with the Public Service Commission via their new web site which is http://www.dps.state.ny.us

All local COCOTS must go through Nynex which is their carrier. The PSC will track them down for you if you can't find the owner. You should have a good chance of resolving your dispute.

Source: Public Service Commission

THE NEW YORK PHONE BOOTH A THING OF THE PAST?

The pay phone in NY goes back to the late 1800's. However, New York Telephone booths (complete with seats and doors) are fast on the road towards extinction. According to Nynex repairmen, they prove too costly to repair, besides the fact that derelicts often use them as toilets.

Many times you'll throw in your quarter only to have it come back to you. This means that the circuit is not operating properly or quite possibly the coin box hasn't been emptied. Worse yet, you may not have the coin come back at all.

NYC traffic makes it impossible to hear well on a street phone, especially at a bus stop. Besides not being able to carry on a normal conversation, you can get a good dose of carbon monoxide as an appetizer.

Generally, hotels, restaurants, bars, and department stores will have access to pay phones where you have a better chance of actually *hearing* your party. These days more and more office buildings have eliminated telephone booths in their lobbies claiming that they attract unnecessary traffic. Some can still be found if you just know where to look. *(See our exclusive list on the next page).*

AVAILABLE INDOOR PHONES AROUND TOWN

Listed below are some of the still surviving indoor Nynex pay phones that in most cases give a dial tone and won't disrupt your ability to hear.

** *Actual telephone booth* *** *Booth with door and seat*	CC Concourse level RL Rear lobby LL Lower lobby OL Outer Lobby L Lobby

BUILDING	LOCATION	STREET	FLOOR
GE Bldg	30 Rockefeller Pl	49-50	9 L
			6 LL
			13 CC
Empire State	33rd & 5th Av		24 L
Lincoln Bldg	60 E. 42	Mad av entr.	15 RL
Citicorp Ctr	153 E. 53rd	Lex Av 53-54	15 CC
200 Park	Vanderbilt Av	44	14 *** L

Paine Weber	1285 Av of Amer	51-52	14CC
			12 ***
1211 Sixth Av		48	12 CC
Woolworth Bldg	233 Broadway	Park Pl	12 RL
Blue Cross Bldg	3 Park Av	34	12 L
Fifth Av Bldg	200 Fifth Av	23	11 L ***
ATT & T Center	Grand Central Sta	42	10 coin
Bank of NY Bldg	80 Broadway		10 L
Chrysler Bldg	42nd & Lexington		8 arcade ***
10 Columbus Cir	58th & B'way		8 L ***
1633 Broadway	50-51		8 LL ***
1400 Broadway	40		7 L **
Courthouse Bldg	60 Centre St		6 L
25 West 43 St	5-6 Aves		6 L
Vanderbilt Ymca	224 E. 47 St	2-3 aves	6 L
Mayflower Hotel	CPW & 61 St		6 L
Surrogates Court	31 Chambers St	Centre st	4 L ***
			2 *** 4 floor
345 Park Avenue	near newstand	51-52	5 L - 4 **
1411 Broadway		39	5 L
West Side Ymca	CPW & 63 St		5 L
Chanin Bldg	122 W 42 St	Lex Ave	5 LL
Assoc Press Bldg	34 W 51 St		4 L **
Time Warner	75 Rockefeller Ct	51-52	4 LL **
630 Fifth Av		50	4 L
555 W 57 St	10th-11th Aves		4 L
2 Park Av		33	4 L
888 7th Av		56-57	4 L
111 Centre St	Cor. White St		4 L
Sony Plaza	550 Madison	55-56	4 arcade
Grace Bldg	43 W. 42 St	6-7 aves	3 RL ***
99 Park Av		40	3 L
Newsweek Bldg	1775 Bway	57-58	3 OL
Fisk Bldg	250 W. 57 St	B'way	3 L
1133 Sixth Av		43	3 L
787 7th Av		51-52	2 OL
1350 Sixth Av		55	2 L

GM Bldg	767 Fifth Av	58-59	2 L
			3 CC
NY Public Library	42 & Fifth Av		all floors ex 3
Mid Manhattan	40 & Fifth Av		all floors ex M
NY Telephone	1166 Sixth Av		No Phones!

NEW YORK FUN FACT

Having trouble getting a phone that works these days? It's not unusual. According to a *NY Times* survey, one third of all pay phones on New York City streets are out of service.

RECENT DEVELOPMENTS

Recently the City Council gave the Department of Information Technology and Telecommunications the right to regulate street phones in New York City. As a result, the companies that operate all pay phones must be registered and pay a $75 fee. Any complaints on street phones go directly to this office. The city has now begun operations to remove all illegal pay phones.

KEY NUMBERS

- *Department of Information Technology and Telecommunications*   718-243-2500

- *Nynex President's Helpline*
Complaints, 24 hrs.   800-722-2300

- *Public Service Commission*   800-342-3377

- *Long Distance Verification*   700-555-4141
  (to identify your carrier)

THE URBAN GUERRILLA

One consumer suggested taking the long distance carriers like AT&T, MCI and Sprint up on their offers to switch. Every time you switch providers accept their cash bonuses, then when another offers better savings, switch again. It's all perfectly legal. However you should be aware of the *Telephone Slamming Scam* listed on page 60.

PART TWO

I CAN'T HEAR

MYSELF SCREAM

AND

OTHER IRRITANTS

"I do have irrefutable evidence that Bigfoot is alive and well ...and living in the apartment right above me."

New York Tenant

#11

WHAT TO DO WITH A NOISY @#$%! NEIGHBOR

The tall slender middle aged man knew he was out of control when he got hold of his old softball bat from the basement of his parent's house. He hadn't used the bat since he was 17 and now at 45 he was clutching it as though he had every intention of putting it to good use.

Only this time he wasn't asked to step up to home plate. Today was payback time. He was planning to use the bat on his neighbor. "I was living right next to a guy who had weekly late night parties. The landlord wouldn't help, the neighbor wouldn't cooperate. It was going on for months," said a tenant who chose to call himself Al "This seemed the only way."

"I've never resorted to violence but I didn't know what else to do," said Al "I spoke to him, wrote him notes -- nothing worked."

Al tried every possible means to rectify the problem, from writing his landlord to writing his assemblyman. He had even once telephoned a radio call-in show hosted by Dr. Bernard Meltzer, an attorney who gave out legal advice to callers. The doctor responded by saying, "That's a tough one. There's not much you can do except move".

At one point the distraught tenant even contacted a psychic healer who tried to change his perception of the problem. That didn't work although the mantra was a catchy tune. Then out of sheer desperation he called the police who intervened, but never with lasting results.

Finally Al phoned his parent's house. His father answered. "Hey dad, you still have my old softball bat?" "Yeah. Why?" his father asked. "I'll be right over for it." "You're not going to do anything stupid are you"? his dad said. There was no reply.

Al remembers taking a mighty swing at his neighbor's door one night. "The dents are still in the door," he remarked. Fortunately the neighbor was not at home.   A relative learning of this actions stopped him from going any further and suggested another way. Al settled for taking out a harassment subpoena which finally led to mediation.   The mediation proved successful and the noisy neighbor moved out. The bat was eventually returned to his parent's basement where it has remained ever since.

As it turns out, I must finally reveal that I was Al, before I became enlightened.   I should also add that whenever I'm feeling depressed all I have to do is look at the dent marks in the door next to my apartment to see just how far I've come.

In New York City one might not know one's neighbor, but you can sure as hell hear them clear as a bell. You've tried slipping notes under their door, in their mailbox, even alerting the super and landlord, who conveniently turn a deaf ear. There's nothing worse in this city than the likes of an inconsiderate louse of a neighbor who refuses to cooperate and lower the volume on their noise exchange.

Noise disruption is a problem that many of us are all too familiar with. Especially when you're up against it on a daily basis. The Council on the Environment is quick to point out that "Stress is the body's response to outside disturbances. A barking dog or a dripping faucet can trigger your body responses: heart rate increases, blood pressure rises, the mouth dries, skin loses color, muscles contract, and blood cholesterol rises."

The New York City Commission of Human Rights, (the standard lease provision) Real Property Law #235 states, *"The landlord or his agent must enforce the right of the tenant to the quiet enjoyment of his/her apartment nuisance free."*

"Bringing a claim against your neighbor for making too much noise is something that is very hard economically to justify" says landlord-tenant attorney Daryl Vernon. "Very often there is no great legal claim to be made for someone making noise." But Mr. Vernon explained that going after your landlord makes better sense because he has greater leverage against your neighbor by means of eviction.

Vernon, who has handled tenant cases in the city, many of which have involved noisy neighbors, went on to say, "When a tenant gets a threat from the landlord he's much more likely to respond because he is in jeopardy of losing the apartment." The landlord is responsible for the warranty of habitability code. When a landlord violates this, a tenant is entitled to get a rent reduction.

Law journals are full of precedent setting cases. In Kalicow Properties vs. Modney, May 2, 1978, the court awarded a 30% abatement of rent because of the landlord's failure to uphold the Warranty of Habitability code requiring a tenant to install a carpet.

Excessive, continuous, and intense noise may be harmful and render an apartment uninhabitable. Other landmark cases include: Rockrose Assoc. vs. Peters, Pekelner vs. Park West Mgmt., Cohen vs. Werner. (All cases accessible via the *New York Law Journal.*)

Real property law #235-b, otherwise known as the *Warranty of Habitability Code* states, *"Every tenant has the right in his apartment and in the building (a) that it be fit for human habitation (b) that it be fit for reasonable uses by the*

*tenant and (c) that it be free from any condition that
endangers or harms the life, health, or safety of the tenant."*

This includes *excessive* noise which besides causing
feelings of profound despair can lead to suicide and murder.
Every year in this country there are noise complaints that
lead to violence. "Studies have demonstrated that
intrusiveness from noisy neighbors has led to aggression,"
says Dr. Arline Bronzaft, a former Professor of Psychology at
City University who has studied the effects of noise.
"Academic studies in the lab tell us that noise increases
aggressive behavior. With people, the press is replete with
incidents of neighbors attacking neighbors."

Consider the case of a Long Island City resident who after
complaining of loud partying was met with laughter from his
neighbors. He returned with a gun and shot several guests
before being escorted to the nearest police station. Or
consider the case cited by Dr., Bronzaft, of a child being shot
in the hallway for making too much noise. There is also the
case of two neighbors in London having committed suicide
because of intrusive noise from neighbors as reported by the
London newspapers. The list goes on and on.

Generally, if you're dealing with a *mensch,* (a Yiddish
term for an "upright and honorable individual") they'll
usually be willing to work with you.   Try to talk it over in a
non-threatening manner without casting blame. Dr. Bronzaft
recommends trying the 'nice approach' by asking the person
to cut down on the noise. "Some people are not aware that
their noise is that intrusive," she says. Extend the courtesy
that you would want extended to yourself.

On the flip side your effort might not improve the
situation at all, this is where things get challenging. Rarely
does the noisemaker think he's doing anything wrong; it's

you who's got the problem.   Human behavior can be extremely difficult to change, especially in an uncooperative jerk.

Perhaps he has all the grace of a thunder lizard when walking across the floor.   Maybe he's the type who causes walls and floors to reverberate when he speaks in a "normal" tone.   Then again he might be the type of individual who laughs as hysterically as a hyena about to go into labor. Better still, he wakes up every morning with the same throat-clearing sounds one would hear at the North American black bear cage in Flushing Meadow Zoo.

Whatever the scenario, the key is not to give up.   There are options at your disposal depending on what kind of noise problem you may have.   As a city dweller residing in a rent stabilized apartment building, I've had to deal with this situation more times than I care to remember.   At best I received marginal or no assistance from a landlord who'd rather have me move out than lift a finger. Of course being a rent stabilized occupant for 20 years might have something to do with it.

Remember, noise is a hard thing to prove because it's all a relative issue.   What's noisy to you may not be so to someone else.   You can't take a photograph of noise but you can get out your cassette recorder and put it on tape.   This issue doesn't quite measure up to the level of murder so the police regard it as low priority.

If, after all your peaceful efforts have been exhausted and you find yourself at the end of your extension cord, consider putting into practice the following measures:

☛ Be fair in your assessment of the noise. Everybody has to put up with some noise in this city. We're not talking about sound sensitive individuals who can hear a pin drop down the hall or those who hear sounds that don't exist. Only you will know whether it's gone too far.

☞ Try to get a fellow neighbor to back up your complaint. There is truth in the saying, "strength in numbers." If you can't find a neighbor who is willing to assist you, don't worry. You can do something about this alone if you are determined to see it through.

☞ Contact your landlord in writing asking for his assistance. (Certified mail return receipt requested is a must!) Leaving a paper trail is imperative.

☞ If the landlord does nothing to help you resolve the problem and it continues, he is responsible for maintaining a private nuisance.

☞ You may withhold your rent until the landlord does something to help you. (Put the rent money aside and remember not to spend it on Chinese takeout!)

☞ Call your local police precinct while the noisemaking is in progress and don't forget to get a signed report from the officers that a disturbance is taking place. Remember, the police consider this a low priority (nuisance) call. Don't expect them to break any speed limits getting there. Be persistent and let them know you are serious. The police make a better appearance than you do.

☞ If all this does not end the noise, bring out the big guns figuratively speaking, of course. Go down to Criminal Court at 346 Broadway (for Manhattan residents; for others see end of chapter) and take out a harassment subpoena against your neighbor. Make sure that your local precinct serves this notice to the guilty party while you are physically present and know when they're home. If it does not do the trick the first time, do it the following week. Don't give up.

☞ You can sue for damages, i.e. loss of sleep, harassment, or the inability to carry out normal activity without interference.   Estimate $20-$100 for every day the disturbance continues.   Keep a log of dates and times when the noise occurs.

☞ You will be given a specific time and date to go to the Mediation Center *(see key numbers section at end of chapter)* as a first step and an alternative to court.

☞ *Don't* contact the DHCR -- Department of Housing and Community Renewal -- hoping that they will help you. This agency moves with all the urgency of glue running down a frozen sidewalk. Don't waste your time with the DHCR on this type of complaint.

Based on first hand experience, the DHCR will only refer your noise problem to Housing Court because this type of problem does not fall under their jurisdiction. In most cases a tenant must make a choice of either going to a city agency to handle their problem, or taking it to Housing Court. Always choose the latter in the case of noise.

Above all, read your lease. Most folks don't. You must see what you're entitled to in long forgotten passages. Looking carefully at your lease can be quite revealing. Above all, remember, if there's hope for the Gaza Strip, there's hope for you too.

Note: Retaliation may not be the most diplomatic of methods but sometimes you might have to make just as much noise as the noisemaker to get their attention. Of course by doing this, you run the risk of further escalating the situation. By and large I personally don't advocate it because it is against the law. However in some instances by those interviewed it has succeeded where other maneuvers have failed. Some dense-heads need to know what it is they have to lose before you can negotiate. Conversely it may invite subsequent retaliation. Be prepared to devote time and energy to the following;

- Purchase a bull horn (AKA Powerhorn) at Radio Shack, model # 32-2038, 10 watt public address unit. This model comes with a built-in siren that sends a loud and clear message. Hold the horn next to your noisemaker's wall or floor, put on the siren and go out for a stroll or do your shopping.

- Wait until you know the noisemakers are asleep and fix two large stereo speakers to their floor or wall from your side. Put on a Jack Hammer drill sound effects tape or CD (available at most record stores). Or put on the soundtrack from "Night of the Living Dead" at full volume and leave your home. Make sure the tape plays continuously. Put your ear plugs in or play it until you can't stand it anymore.

If your prefer, give your neighbor a dose of their own medicine by driving a 20 penny nail into the wall that separates the two of you. Attach a violin string to the nail. Pull the string tight and with your other hand run a violin bow across it. The wall will act as a conduit for the horrendous noise that follows.

GET A GRIP

☞ Manhattan Mediation Center (for other boroughs see end of chapter) at 346 Broadway is a state and city center that resolves disputes ranging from harassment, assault and mischief to aggravated assault. It provides an alternative to both civil and criminal court without charge.

☞ The resolutions reached are put in writing and signed by all parties involved, with trained mediators negotiating fair and for the most part, abiding solutions. You will not have to wait long to have your problem heard by a mediator. The turn-around time here is approximately 1 week. Mediators are lawyers, ex-cops, teachers and security guards.

☞ Bear in mind that the other party will not need to be physically present at the mediation, since this is a voluntary measure. However they might be more inclined to respond when you have two police officers from your local precinct physically serve them with the summons. Be warned that on some occasions it might take more than one visit to get the message across.

☞ The MMC boasts a high success rate of 87% in resolving matters and yet New Yorkers are not even aware of their existence. It is a step you can do for yourself without expense, short of taking time off from work. It's also a viable alternative to hiring an attorney for civil court.

☞ Have witnesses to excessive noise and be prepared to get notarized statements from them if they can't be present in court. Remember, it's always better to have them appear. The stronger the proof, the better your chances of prevailing.

☞ If your problem continues and your landlord still refuses to help, contact your local assemblyperson or councilperson; they can be of assistance communicating on your behalf.

☞ In the meantime, invest in a small device for your apartment known as *"The Quiet Machine."* This is an anti- noise pollution device, similar to a white noise generator and is programmed to produce a quiet and relaxing sound. It helps block out a good deal of noise filtering in, especially conversation, piano playing, and foot thumping.

For further info on *"The Quiet Machine"* write:
First & Co., PO Box 916, Dept. G, Forest Hills, NY 11375.

KEY NUMBERS

TENANT NOISE

- *Council on the Environment Noise Committee*
  Dr. Arline Bronzaft   212-288-7532

- *Bronx: Institute for Mediation & Conflict Resolution*
  391 East 149th Street, Suite 407
  Bronx, NY 10455   718-585-1190

- *Brooklyn: Brooklyn Mediation Center*
  210 Joralemon Street, Room 618
  Brooklyn, NY 11201   718-834-6671

- *Manhattan: Manhattan Mediation Center*
  346 Broadway, Suite 400W
  New York, NY 10013   212-577-1740

- *Queens: Queens Mediation Network*
  89-64 163rd Street
  Jamaica, NY 11432   718-523-6868

- *Staten Island: Staten Isl. Community Dispute Ctr.*
  42 Richmond Terrace
  Staten Island, NY 10301   718-720-9410

- *DHCR Dept. Of Housing-Community Renewal*
  Queens   718-739-6400
- *DHCR Manhattan*   212-240-6010

- *Tenants Rights*   519-5797
                                            903-9500
(for tenants of rent-controlled and rent stabilized apartments)

- *Metropolitan Council on Housing*   693-0550
198 Broadway
(advises you of your rights as a tenant)

- *Housing Preservation & Development*   960-4800
(No heat, hot water or required repairs - Open 24 hrs.)

- *NYS Tenant & Neighborhood Coalition*   695-8922
(Tenants guide to subletting and apartment sharing)

- *Citizens Committee for New York*   989-0909
(Organizing a block association, grants and grass roots training)

- *Civil Court Line*   791-6000

COMMERCIAL NOISE COMPLAINTS

Communities all across the city deal with noisy establishments in place of individuals from time to time.

The Rowdy Bar Bill (S-6863) sponsored by State Senator Catherine Abate gives the community more leverage with the State Liquor Authority's ability to "discipline and punish offending establishments". It has passed both houses and been signed into law by the Governor as of August 1996.

NEW QUALITY OF LIFE HOTLINE

Contact the newly established Quality of Life Hotline at 888-677-LIFE and sound off.

KEY NUMBERS

COMMERCIAL NOISE

* Patron Disturbances, Rowdiness   417-4069
  (State Liquor Authority) Also local police precinct

* Traffic Congestion, Double Parking   262-4343
  Dept. Of Transportation
  Div. Traffic Intelligence

* Building Complaints   312-8000
  Department of Buildings

* Overcrowding or Unsafe Conditions - (Contact your
  local firehouse and State Liquor Authority)

Attorneys specializing in Landlord-Tenant problems

Daryl Vernon   261 Madison Ave.   949-7300
Belkin, Burden   342 Madison Ave.   867-4466

NEW YORK FUN FACT

In an effort to cut down on commercial noise and air pollution, sightseeing helicopters will no longer be permitted to fly over Manhattan. Under a new stipulation, copter tours must now fly primarily over the East and Hudson Rivers at an altitude of at least 1,500 feet according to the Federal Aviation Administration.

Choppers flying illegally can be reported to the Eastern Region Helicopter Council at (888)-374-2463

"My contention for less noise is based on the experience and observation of nearly 20 years practice of my profession in New York City. And I am satisfied that the irritation caused by the din in which we live today is essentially health-destroying and plays no unimportant part in predicting disease of the brain and nervous system, and delaying the recovery of the sick."

John H. Girdner

#12

North American Review
September 1896

THE TAMING OF THE SHRIEK
UNATTENDED AUTO ALARMS

A police officer responding to numerous complaints on 72nd Street was asked by a passerby why he wouldn't ticket a car whose alarm went unattended for more than 45 minutes. "As far as I'm concerned this is the same as jaywalking. It's at my discretion. Besides..." he continued. "I don't have any tickets." He got back into his patrol car and waited for a back-up crew while the alarm sounded for 20 more agonizing minutes. The passerby was aghast. "Whoever heard of a police officer with no tickets?" he muttered to himself.

Not satisfied with the answer he received he brought the matter to the attention of the commanding officer at the 20th precinct. Surprisingly, the Captain defended the officer. "This officer acted properly," stated Captain Perlov authoritatively. When the passerby took exception and cited the new law governing unattended auto alarms that empowers the police not only to ticket the vehicle but to disconnect the alarm, the precinct commander admitted that she was not familiar with it. Herein was the problem. How could the community expect the police to enforce a law that they had no knowledge of?

"Auto alarms are the New York equivalent to the cricket," says comedian Jeff Stilson. If you spend any time in New York, you're familiar with these piercing wails that go off at any hour of the day or night with all the tact of an elephant seal in heat.

"Some car owners are considerate. They install the kind of alarm that plays not only 1 but a medley of 4 different shrieks just so that the rest of us won't get bored," says community activist Ben Solowitz. "Just when you think the alarm finally stops - it starts up all over again."

Insurance companies do offer lower rates for owners of cars equipped with alarms which help explain why they're so pervasive. However, there are many who feel they're a worn out cliché whose time has passed. Move over Edsel, Pet Rock, and Nehru suit. Seems the only thing car alarms successfully achieve are driving people crazy and making New Yorkers into ex-New Yorkers.

"Let's be candid", one long time resident remarked. "When you hear one of these alarms go off do you suddenly run to see what happened or do you just cuss out the owner for not turning the damn thing off?"

In 1992, the Goodman-Grannis law, bill senate 6392-D, now 399-U of Gen. Bus. Law, was passed by the State Legislature which imposed a point-of-sale restriction on alarms to a 3-minute time limit.

Today the police may tell you that they can't do anything about this problem but it's probably because their precinct commanders don't require them to be aware of quality-of-life laws on the books. The truth is that they not only have the power to issue a summons ranging from $175 to $700 per violation, but that they also have the authority to <u>disconnect</u> the alarm thanks to a new law in effect.

Local law 24-221 of the NYC administrative code now gives the police the legal clout, much to their chagrin. This legislation was introduced by Councilmember Stanley Michels of District #7, signed into law by outgoing mayor David Dinkins and became New York City law as of April 1994.

Yet as Councilmember Andrew Eristoff, who co-sponsors much of the quality-of-life legislation in New York City has discovered, the problem lies in enforcement. When he asked an officer why he didn't hand out a ticket to a bicycle messenger who shouldn't have been on the sidewalk, the officer stated, "I don't have the right summons book." "The police can't issue a regular summons for many of these violations," says Eristoff. "It must be a special ECB (Environmental Control Board) summons."

Eristoff believes, "the next step is to get a unified summons because many police don't want to have to carry around a second book of tickets on their belt." Precinct commanders let it slide as well. Is this what a police officer means when they say they have "no tickets?"

Another contributing factor is that the police aren't required to carry 'Slim Jims' (a lock-picking tool) which allows them, as well as other city agencies, i.e. Dept. Of Transportation, to enter the vehicle in violation. However, if your car is illegally parked -- watch how quickly they get into it to have it towed. The $200 incentive for the City might just have something to do with it.

GET A GRIP

- The law gives the police the right to have cars whose alarms have sounded in excess of 3 minutes, towed away, disconnected and ticketed.

- When you do call the precinct, ask for the name of the officer answering the phone. If you receive a less than helpful response or a 'we can't do anything about it' response, ask to speak with the desk sergeant. Remember to follow up. It helps to know the name of the precinct commander.

- Write a brief note telling of your experience and make sure you send a copy of it to the Police Commissioner of the City of New York at 1 Police Plaza, New York 10038. If you're still madder than hell, call your local councilperson and local community board. (see chapter 36)

- Find out from your precinct commander what they are doing to make sure that their officers are aware of relevant quality-of-life laws and whether they are carrying around the required summonses.

Still another obstacle to overcome is that the NYPD considers this type of complaint *a nuisance call* or *low priority*. In years past, when the police did disable alarms, they were sued by the owners of the cars for damages. Presently it comes as no surprise that these calls now have all the urgency of a prickly heat telethon. It may take literally hours before the police arrive and one can only hope that the car battery will poop out before you pass out.

☞ I also recommend attending the next police community council meeting at your local precinct. These meetings are held monthly and attended by precinct Captains. It's a good way for them to be aware of what's going on right under their noses. The idea here is to get their attention with your gripe.

☞ There is also the Office of Public Advocate at your disposal. If quality of life laws are on the books, they should be enforced against those who break it.

☞ The police (unwilling as they may seem) must locate the owner of the vehicle through a license plate check when the alarm exceeds 3 minutes.

It's The Law!

24-221 (d) New York Administrative Code "No Owner of a building or of a motor vehicle shall have in operation an audible burglar alarm thereon unless such burglar alarm shall be capable of and shall automatically terminate its audible response within 15 minutes of its being activated in the case of a building, and 3 minutes of its being activated in the case of a motor vehicle."

BLOWING OFF STEAM

I know of one irate citizen who was so incensed by the recent onslaught of shrieking cars in his neighborhood that he made up his own 8"x11" adhesive signs that he pasted directly on the windshield of   any unattended ear-deafening auto as an alternative to smashing it.

In very direct language he told the owners of such cars what inconsiderate louses they were for being irresponsible. He discovered that this helped lower his blood pressure for the moment anyway.

WARNING

YOUR CAR ALARM IS CREATING AN
UNNECESSARY DISTURBANCE
TO THE INHABITANTS OF THIS
NEIGHBORHOOD.

THE ONLY THING STOPPING SOME OF US
FROM SMASHING IN YOUR WINDSHIELD IS THE
GOODNESS IN OUR HEARTS.

HOWEVER, ALL THINGS CONSIDERED,
DON'T COUNT ON IT!

ARRANGE TO HAVE YOUR ALARM
SHUT OFF AFTER 3 MINUTES OR ELSE!

IT'S THE LAW!

THE URBAN
GUERRILLA

Seems a disgruntled neighbor on the Upper West Side got his point across (Guerrilla style) in the dead of winter. A car with New Jersey license plates whose alarm wailed throughout the night was pelted with at least one dozen eggs that froze overnight. Full page notes were plastered on the car telling the owner what would be done if the incessant shrieking were to continue. The resident promised to leave a "present" if there was to be a next time. Needless to say, there wasn't a next time, (at least not with Jersey license plates anyway.)

If the local police are having a difficult time remembering what their responsibilities are with your next unattended car alarm incident, why not remind them what was dispatched from Police Plaza headquarters not too long ago: *(see next page.)*

NEW YORK FUN FACT

State Senator Catherine Abate (D) wants to introduce legislation that would take some irresponsible car owners to task. Law breakers who allow their cars to wail over the 3 minute time limit would have their discounted theft insurance reduced by a minimum of 30%.

INTERIM ORDER

Number 51
Ref. P.G. ** 109

TO ALL COMMANDS

Subject: PROCEDURE FOR HANDLING VEHICLES WHOSE ALARMS FAIL TO CEASE WITHIN THREE (3) MINUTES OR THAT HAVE IN OPERATION AN AUDIBLE STATUS INDICATOR.

1.   Effective March 29, 1994, Section 24-221 (d) of the Administrative Code of the City of New York was amended pursuant to Local Law 110 of 1993. The new law requires that an audible vehicle alarm cease to sound within three (3) minutes after being activated. Additionally, the same section also provides that no audible burglar alarm on a motor vehicle shall be capable of being activated except:

a. By direct physical contact with that motor vehicle, or
b. Through the use of an individual remote activation that is designed to be used with the audible burglar alarm system of a particular vehicle which alarm shall be audible of and shall terminate its audible response within three (3) minutes of being activated.

Section 24-221(e) provides that no owner of a motor vehicle shall have in operation an audible status indicator on such motor vehicle.

2.   Section 1640 of the New York State Vehicle and Traffic Law (V.T.L.) and Section 1404 of the New York City Charter have also been amended to allow for the service of an Environmental Control Board "Notice of Violation and Hearing" (E.C.B. Summons) for violation of Section 24-221.

3.   Therefore, uniformed members of the service assigned to investigate audible vehicle alarms will comply with the following procedure:

PURPOSE

To take enforcement action when an audible vehicle alarm is activated and ceases to sound within three (3) minutes or when an audible status indicator is operated on a vehicle.

DEFINITION

AUDIBLE STATUS INDICATOR - For the purpose of this procedure, any sound reproduction device on a motor vehicle that emits or causes to be emitted any continuous or near continuous sound for the purpose of warning that an audible burglar alarm has been installed on such motor vehicle and is operational or for creating the appearance that such an alarm has been installed on such motor vehicle and is operational.

PROCEDURE

When a uniformed member of the service is notified or becomes aware that an audible vehicle alarm has been activated or audible status indicator has been activated and the vehicle is parked on a public highway or in a parking lot open to the public:

UNIFORMED

MEMBER OF

THE SERVICE

1. Make entry in ACTIVITY LOG (PD112-145) of time when the member first observed the audible alarm
2. Comply with the provisions of Patrol Guide procedure 117-19, "Deactivation of Motor Vehicle Alarms."
3. Take all reasonable steps to disconnect alarm or indicator without damaging the vehicle.
4. Prepare a Environmental Control Board "Notice of Violation and Hearing" for violation of the Administrative Code Section 24-221 (d) (alarm) or Section 24-221 (e) (audible status indicator).
A. Enter N-12 in box captioned VIOLATION CODE
B. Enter $175.00 in box captioned MAILABLE PENALTY SCHEDULE
C. Enter $700.00 in box captioned MAXIMUM PENALTY FOR VIOLATION.

"Can you turn that crap up? I still got one eye socket left."
                                                    Nick Di Paolo
                                                    Stand-Up Comic

#13

BLASTING BOOM BOXES

Tony Giordono was the Rodney Dangerfield of Sheepshead Bay. He got no respect. Repeated phone calls to the police about youngsters across the street from his home blasting their car radios, fell on deaf ears. "By the time the cops finally did come around -- the kids had taken off but not before blowing out my ear canals," he said. "I wasn't planning to start a confrontation when I was out numbered. To make it short," he continued. "I didn't want to be tomorrow's headline on the New York Post."

However when things got out of control, Tony discovered another solution. He'd put on his dark colored clothes against the night sky and would journey to the roof of his five story apartment house. It was there that he'd reach into his reserve and withdraw what he called his "Old Reliable." On every Halloween back in the old neighborhood, city buses and trucks passing by were usually great targets for an onslaught of water balloons and eggs.

"I never thought that at 45, I'd still be tossin' 'em," he said. With deadly accuracy he'd launch his assault against the loud vehicles. But not before waiting until they exceeded the 10 minute grace period. Once the rap and salsa continued, a red flag went up. "At least if they had played the oldies it would have been more tolerable," he said. According to Giordono, the blasting boom boxers never did figure where the launchings came from because his block was surrounded by tall buildings. After a few offensives, the boom boxers usually got the message and headed for the nearest car wash.

Noise is simply not an annoyance. It is a health hazard -- plain and simple," states Dr. Arline Bronzaft of the Council on the Environment's Noise Committee. Being continually exposed to noise can do wonders for your nervous system. It destroys the cells in the inner ear. Cells that do not regenerate. Our hearing deteriorates every time we are exposed to extended periods of intense sound. Hearing loss that is caused by noise is permanent and incurable.

Noise in New York? So what else is new? The difference now is there might be some relief on the way from the Department of Environmental Protection. The DEP has been working closely with the police department on issuing summonses to those motorists who refuse to lower the volume on their hot rod mega-woofers. "Vehicles with boom box speakers blasting away are a violation of the Motor Vehicle Law," states Ian Michaels, a spokesman for the DEP. Although the difficult part may be catching mobile units committing the act, sound trap operations are now underway. In a recent year nearly 150 vehicles blasting away were seized by the police department.

Bill S.2187 of the Motor Vehicle Law (passed in 1996) prohibits noise from any car radio or boom box which exceeds 70 decibels from at least 25 feet away. If the source is in violation, the vehicle or radio may be confiscated by the police on the spot. The owner can be left to either walk or worse yet, take a New York City subway home. "In many instances drugs and weapons are discovered in the vehicles," said Michaels.

The DEP is a complaint-driven agency that can enforce the New York City Noise Code via sound trap operations. However the DEP does not have equipment to enforce moving vehicle violations. The police must be involved in that process. On a weekend in Greenwich Village, a police car spots a speeding car with ear-deafening speakers pass MacDougal Street heading east where an inspector is positioned at a stakeout. He measures the noise with a sound-level meter.

Discovering a violation, he radios the police car positioned up on Broadway that a red Chevy jeep is "pumping the volume." The cops head off the car, issue a summons and confiscate the vehicle.

WHAT TO DO

☛ Notify the Department of Environmental Protection of a noise problem that is from a stationary source, call *718-DEP-HELP.*

☛ Make sure you follow up about a week later to see what was done.

☛ If, on the other hand the source of the noise is from people or mobile units, and you're madder than hell, let your local commanding officer know about it.

NEW YORK FUN FACT

There were 332 autos confiscated citywide by the Police Department for loud stereos in 1995.

Source: NYPD

GET A GRIP

- Make sure your local precinct is trained in the use of sound level meters and that their officers are equipped with ECB (Environmental Control Board) summonses that are specifically called for on this type of violation.

- Motorcyclists: It is illegal in New York State to have a "Straight Pipe" on your bike. This feature enables the bike to shatter one's eardrums with loud, ear-splitting sounds. Now this piece of equipment joins the ranks as a violation the NYC Motor Vehicle Code. In a 35 M.P.H. zone, the noise from a motorcycle cannot exceed 70 decibels at 25 feet or the police can issue a $100 summons on the spot.

- Up to now, the DEP inspectors have had to travel with the police. Inspectors got an accurate reading on the sound-level meter, the police took it from there. However Mr. Micahels of the DEP states that more and more police officers are being trained on how to use sound level meters on their own. Consequently, more fines can be handed out.

- If your neighborhood is being besieged by a blitzkrieg of car speaker noise, it pays to put the heat on your local precinct to enforce the noise code. One effective way is to bring it to the attention of your local community board and your local legislators. (See pgs. 259-271 & pgs. 326-7)

- The chain of command at your local precinct needs to know that your neighborhood means business. Every year the DEP trains police officers in the use of sound-level meters. Contact your precinct commander and recommend it. It pays to organize and put the pressure on your local precinct -- so get your neighbors to join in on complaints or go to your local block association. "Quality of Life" and "New York City," are terms that don't need to be mutually exclusive.

In October, 1994, Police Commissioner Bratton realigned local precincts by enabling precinct Captains to better serve the city by virtue of their authority. The Super Chiefs at your local precincts now are high ranking inspectors with more power to run their own operations. Currently they have far more power than their predecessors, instead of having to get approval from the chain of command for every procedure.

In their possession are more crime-fighting tools such as recording devices, sound-level meters, as well as their own buy-and-bust and anti-car theft operations.

NEW YORK NOISE

(Hearing loss begins at about 90 dcb)

Quiet home	20 decibels
Normal talking	40
Rooster crow	45
Car hyperbass speakers	65 +
Car alarm	80
Garbage truck	85
Jackhammer	88
Shouting	90
Discotheques	95
Inside No. 1 Train	102.8
Gun fired near ear	160

Source: Department of Environmental Protection

Get A Grip: If you must raise your voice to speak to someone only 3 feet away, then your immediate environment could be hazardous to your health.

KEY NUMBERS

- *Mayor's Community Assistance Unit*   788-7418

- *To find out your local precinct*   374-5000

- *Dept. of Environmental Protection*   718-DEP-HELP
  (complaints, information)

IF THIS HOTLINE IS COLD --- CALL:

- *DEP Commissioner's office*   718-595-6567

- *League for the Hard of Hearing*   255-1932

- *F.A.N.N.Y.*   229-0202
  Friends Against Noisy New York
  (ask for free newsletter)

(Contact your local Community Board as well.
For further info see pgs. 326-327)

#14

GET OUT THE WET SUIT --
IT'S ANOTHER WATER MAIN BREAK

If the Lincoln Center fountain is off and you're in need of a great shot to send the folks back home, you may be in time for your first water main break in New York City. When this does occur you want to have the Instamatic handy because this is a sight you're not likely to forget.

Telephone lines, subway service, bus routes, and businesses will cease to function. For New Yorkers this might be yet another reason to hit happy hour at the nearest watering hole. Sometimes knowing when to surrender isn't such a bad thing.

THE NITTY GRITTY DETAILS

A water main is a tunnel or pipe that carries either drinking water or water for fire hydrants and sinks. New York City has all together, 5,814 miles of water mains that run throughout all five boroughs. During the last decade, an average of 500-600 water mains broke each year according to city officials.

The reasons for a water main break are varied. It could be that the pipe is very old, not very old, or that vibrations from subways and city traffic may have stressed or weakened the main. Corrosive soil and street excavations are also contributing factors to a pipe that is already fatigued and stressed out. Believe it or not, in some cases an old water main can be more stable than a new one. After 1970, the city began using a stronger metal to avoid as many ruptures.

GET A GRIP

- If you see something developing into a water main break, call the New York City Department of Environmental Protection, not to be confused with its federal counterparts. The DEP's 24 hour communication hot line for water main breaks, leaky fire hydrants, sewer backups, clogged catch basins, and leaky city pipes is 718-DEP-HELP.

- After calling to report a break, reward yourself by going to a movie. Perhaps have some sushi, or if you really hit the jackpot, your boss will let you go home early when he discovers his main frame suddenly floating down Broadway.

KEY NUMBER

- *Dept. of Environmental Protection*   718-DEP-HELP
  Emergencies, 24 hr. line

3 Reasons Why Alligators Can't Live in New York City Sewers

①   Alligators are cold-blooded creatures and cannot survive in the winter.

②   An alligator *needs* air to breathe. That is not possible after it rains and a NY sewer fills up.

③   There is not enough food in a NYC sewer to feed a full size gator. Besides, New York has the toughest sewer rats in the country.

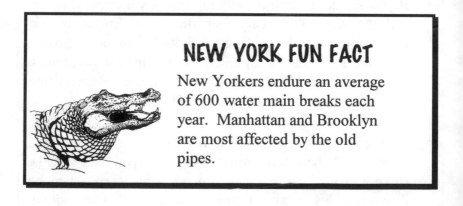

NEW YORK FUN FACT

New Yorkers endure an average of 600 water main breaks each year. Manhattan and Brooklyn are most affected by the old pipes.

THE URBAN GUERRILLA

Once the water pressure in your neighborhood is restored, you should take precautions by boiling any water used in the preparation of food for at least 3 minutes.

Ice cubes should *only* be made with boiled water.

When washing dishes in soap and hot water, it is advisable to soak them for several minutes in a solution made up of one capful chlorine bleach per gallon of water. Air dry.

PART THREE

DON'T YOU HATE IT

WHEN THAT

HAPPENS?

#15

GREATEST UNSOLVED MYSTERIES OF MANHATTAN ISLAND

A puzzling array of everyday phenomena for the New Yorker to ponder:

The guy in the seat next to you on the subway is sitting with his legs in different time zones while your house keys are digging into your thigh. On your left sits a woman singing out-of-tune to her Walkman. *(Do these idiots work in teams or should I just introduce them to each other?)*

When you're waiting for a bus -- why does the bus coming in the opposite direction always arrive first? *(These guys must have one helluva jet stream.)*

On the telephone: You get a busy signal for two and a half hours -- then finally you get through and no one answers. *(Per chance did they pass out from talking so long?)*

Why is it when you go to an empty rest room and pick the last of many booths for privacy -- that the person entering next invariably parks themselves down in the booth <u>right</u> next to yours? *(Are they lonely or has this suddenly turned into a contest?)*

Where do they come from?   Those short elderly women, usually around 4'11'', who always claim to be smelling gas? *(Are they talking utility company gas or the other kind?)*

Why does the utility company always begin drilling directly under your window at 8 a.m. sharp on the one morning you can sleep late? *(And can they drill just a little bit louder? I can still feel my pulse.)*

Who are these senior citizens you see removing signs from corner bus stops? Like clock work, once a day there's some strange bird whose sole mission in life is to rip off flyers and announcements the rest of us put up. *(I'd be willing to bet they're the same folks who liked "Ishtar.")*

You lay down sixteen dollars on a movie for you and your date, after standing in line for forty-five minutes during a hail storm. Yet you always manage to pick the two seats in the whole theater directly in front of the one idiot whose idea of a fun evening is to kick the back of your seat. *(Does he by any chance know the guy who tears off signs at the bus stop?)*

Why, in the middle of a conversation do some people say, "ya know?" when we, listening, <u>don't</u> know?

How come drivers like to overheat a NYC bus in winter until you're ready to disrobe and have a luau in Penn Station?

When you're drinking from the office water fountain: why does the stream of water going into your mouth suddenly make an abrupt jump when someone flushes the toilet? *(Suddenly I think I'll use the Coke machine.)*

What knucklehead decided to call it the "Express Line" at the supermarket when it takes the cashier half an hour to ring up three rolls of toilet paper and a jar of pickles? Then you always manage to get the one that screams, "I need singles!"

Why do they put bus stops directly over subway gratings, just where you'll be counting your change?

When you dine at a restaurant by yourself, why does the hostess always have a smirk on her face when she says, "Just one?"

You don't get a phone call all day. But the moment you're standing with your pants down around your ankles in the bathroom...

People with backpacks on crowded buses. Why aren't they required to be registered with the state and have rear view mirrors? *(I say send them back to Jersey where they belong.)*

#16

ANNOYANCE AND OBSCENE PHONE CALLS

According to the Annoyance Call Bureau, over 181,500 annoying and obscene calls were made in a recent year and in just the 212 area code alone. State figures rise to 726,000 and these are just the calls that are reported!

If you find yourself on the receiving end, changing your number is not necessarily a cure, since more than 75% of these calls come from someone you know, says The Annoyance Call Bureau.

Making repeated, harassing, obscene, or threatening calls is against the law. Here's what to do if you find yourself on the receiving end:

GET A GRIP

- Don't respond to the caller at all. It is important to remember that the caller is looking for a reaction from you.

- Simply hang up and then press *57 (or dial 1157 if you have a rotary phone) and stay on the line. Wait for the recording which will tell you that the call has been traced. Nynex will record the caller's phone number, date, and time. This feature will even allow you to trace an unpublished number.

- Once you have traced at least two calls, contact your local police precinct to file a complaint. Call 1-800-332-6963 and leave the complaint number and the name of the officer who will be handling the call on the voice mail. Nynex will then open a case for you.

- If Nynex traces two or more calls back to the same number, they will in turn notify the police where the calls are originating from.

The information gathered by the phone company is *only* released to the police. *57 is stored by Nynex for a period of 90 days without a police complaint number. However, once a police complaint number is received, your case will remain open for up to three years.

You may want to consider taping the call with the 2-way record feature on your answering machine and keeping it on file for the police.

The Nynex company (your local phone carrier) now utilizes features that can help alleviate annoying calls.

- *Caller ID* - Identifies and displays the caller's number
- *Caller ID with Name Service* - Identifies and displays both the caller's number as well as their name
- *Per-Call Blocking Service* - Blocks the display of your number and name on a Caller ID box for a *single* call when you dial *67 before dialing the number
- *All-Call Blocking Service* - Blocks display of your number and name on a Caller ID box for *every* call.
- *Anonymous Call Rejection* - Will not accept any incoming call unless their number is identified.

HOW TO GET RELIEF WITH
ANNOYING TELEMARKETING CALLS

Telemarketers make 100 million calls a week and generate 280 billion dollars a year. The "Center for the Study of Commercialism," a group against persistent telemarketers, states that there is a now an effective way one can retaliate against those who don't take "no" for an answer on the telephone. A recent survey also tells us that 7 out of 10 of us consider telemarketing an invasion of privacy.

Under State and Federal law, persons making telephone calls to consumers must identify themselves, the individual or business they represent, the purpose of the call, and the nature of the goods or services they are selling. They are only permitted to call between the hours of 8 am and 9 p.m.

If you tell a telemarketer to put you on their "Do Not Call" list, tell them to send written confirmation. Also keep accurate records of when they ignored your request. You could collect a settlement against the firm. Lawsuits may be filed with the Attorney General's office or by any individual who receives any subsequent calls.

The Telephone Consumer Protection Act (TCPA), passed by Congress in 1992, requires the Federal Trade Commission to establish a system for listing people who don't want to receive unsolicited sales calls. If telemarketers ignore this command it could mean $500 for the first violation and as much as $1500 for subsequent offenses.

According to experts, one should write a brief letter to the firm and tell them to stop calling. Also request a copy of their *Do Not Call Policy.* If they continue, you need to follow up with the Attorney General's office. By Federal law, firms must maintain a "Do Not Call" list. For more information and a "Stop The Calls" kit, send $3 to: CSC, 1875 Connecticut Avenue NW, Suite 300, Washington, DC 20009.

THE URBAN
GUERRILLA

Near your phone always have handy a referee's whistle just
for those special occasions. Give the obscene phone caller a
screeching ear-splitting blast right into the phone. A
musician friend possessed an even better weapon
-- his trumpet. All he had to do was hit a high C into the
receiver. Needless to say, he was never bothered again.

KEY NUMBERS:

- *Annoyance Call Bureau (recording)* 890-6200

- *Private Citizen* (organization devoted to ending
  telephone pollution)   800-CUT-JUNK

- *NYNEX Privacy Line*   800-322-3436

NEW YORK FUN FACT

Computer, telemarketing, misdirected hang up calls and
unsolicited faxes are not against the law. If you've reached
the end of your telephone cord and wish to request that your
name not appear on any of telemarketer's lists write: *Direct
Market Association, Telephone Preference Service, P.O. Box
9014, Farmingdale, NY 11735-9014*

#17

WHAT TO DO IF YOUR CAR GETS TOWED

You double-parked, just ducked into the newsstand for your weekly lottery ticket and BINGO you hit the jackpot with the City of New York -- you got nailed! Either your car is now in the process of being hooked up to one of the 130 city tow trucks or it's already traveling downtown on a short leash.

Up until recently, you stood a very small chance of getting your car unhooked once it was immobilized by a tow operator. Thanks to a new law, if you've been towed in midtown between 34th-60th streets, from 3rd to 8th Aves., and you find your car already hooked to a police truck, the operator will be required to release it thanks to the *Field Release Program.* In other boroughs, once it's hooked it will be taken away.

A motorist will have to pay a "field release penalty" of $75, as well as the parking ticket once you show your registration or insurance card. This applies to a violation tow, not a *target* tow, i.e. one that is supervised by the Police Dept.

If you are one of the more than 100,000 motorists who have discovered their car missing or suddenly see it waving bye-bye, you know why this is listed as one the most aggravating and pervasive New York City hassles.

☛   First and Foremost: If you don't see your car on the street call 212-TOW-AWAY. Getting towed below 96th street means that your vehicle will very likely be waiting for you at Pier 76. The Pier is located at West 38th Street and 12th Avenue, aka the Main Pound, open 7 days a week.

☛ Call the Parking Violations Bureau (477-4430) to check and see if there are any outstanding tickets you haven't paid. Be prepared to call at your leisure since you'll more than likely get a busy signal. (see end of chapter.)

MOST COMMON REASONS FOR GETTING TOWED;

☹ Misreading or misunderstanding the parking sign
☹ Parking in a school-parking zone
☹ Taking a chance by ducking in a store for a few seconds
☹ Parking on the wrong side during alternate-side days
☹ Double-parking
☹ Blocking a bus lane, fire hydrant or intersection

TOWING BY BOROUGH

	Manhattan	Bronx, Brooklyn, Queens
No Standing	4,708	1,777
No Parking	1,913	1,185
Fire Hydrant	669	774
Double Parking	143	319
Bus Lane	265	182
Other	503	319
TOTAL	8,198	4,556

*No Department of Transportation Tow Operations in Staten Island
Source: DOT 11/94

Many motorists ask why the DOT makes hard-to-read parking signs that make little or no sense. According to those at the DOT, priority to commercial vehicles and the scarcity of curb space contribute to the confusing and unintelligible restrictions. (How's that for an evasive answer?)

If your car is already en route to the garage it will be difficult to stop the tow. However, if you dispute the tow, you have the right to request the tow operator's supervisor on the scene. The driver must comply.

Exceptions in towing do arise from extraordinary circumstances. A supervisor does have the authority to release your vehicle based solely on their discretion. An extraordinary circumstance can range anywhere from medical reasons, going into labor, handling an armful of babies or quite possibly being carried off by a flying reptile at noon with a nail in your shoe.

The Department of Transportation has now set up a new hotline for traffic complaints (7 am-7 pm) **CALL DOT**

The police department is now in charge of towing cars in New York City. Formerly the DOT did not encourage their operators to tow a vehicle that is left standing with an animal in it, assuming that the animal can be seen. This does not mean to suggest that you immediately run out and get a stuffed rotweiler to plant in the front seat. But it does remain an exception. If you do leave your animal be sure to keep your windows open a couple of inches each.

WHAT TO EXPECT
ONCE YOU GET DOWN THERE

These days a customer service representative at the main pound will meet, greet, and help explain procedures when you arrive. If you need to retrieve anything from your car, you'll need to be escorted to your vehicle.

If on the other hand you have any outstanding parking tickets, rest assured that you will not even get as far as customer service. Instead, you will be directed to the Parking Violations Bureau where you must settle up first. Expect to come all the way back to Pier 76 *after* you've done all that. So remember to call the PVB first.

If you have all of the following, plan on being there for the next 45 minutes or so. This pound is no longer open 24 hours a day. New hours are 7 am-11 p.m., Monday through Friday. On some Fridays it is open 24 hours, and 7 am-7 p.m., Saturdays. Closed on Sunday.

① *Registration for your vehicle*
② *Driver's license*
③ *Either $150 in cash, traveler's checks, certified check or a NYCE bank card that can be used to debit your account in the amount of the tow only.*

(Company checks are acceptable only if they are for commercial vehicles, provided you have a notarized letter and company ID.)

GET A GRIP

- If you feel as though you've been wronged and want to appeal the tow, you have the right to do so with the PVB at 1 Centre Street in Manhattan. It is advisable that you don't go in person unless you have loads of time to kill and want to catch up on your reading. It is for sure that you will be kept waiting. What I suggest is to appeal the summons by *mail*. If successful in your appeal, you will have the summons as well as the tow reversed and any money will be refunded to you.

- The best advice from people who have gone through this totally forgettble experience is -- *"When in doubt about where to park, put your vehicle in the garage. It's cheaper than paying $150."*

- It is best to avoid peak hours usually 1-7 PM. In any event it is advisable that you bring something to read. Keep in mind that there is a $15 a day storage fee after 24 hours. After just 96 hours, if no one claims a vehicle, it is considered abandoned and gets to go on the auction block after just thirty days.

TARGET TOWING

Target tows work with other city agencies (Taxi and Limousine Commission, Transit Authority, Department of Motor Vehicles, Department of Consumer Affairs) and focus on either unlicensed or uninsured drivers. Target tows also single out vehicles that are uninspected. According to the DOT, 40% of drivers fall into at least one of the above-mentioned categories.

SCOFF TOWING

If you have three or more unpaid parking tickets totaling at least $150, you will be considered a scofflaw. Your vehicle will be towed and impounded by the Sheriff or Marshall's office.

Once tracked down by the PVB's computer system, known as S.T.A.R.S., your vehicle will be towed and impounded. All vehicles seized are videotaped by the Sheriff in the event of a claim for damages. If they do damage your car in the process, they'll repair it without charge (be prepared to prove it with photographs, etc.) If you don't claim your car here after 23 days at the Main Pound, it is "officially" eligible to be auctioned off.

TOP 10 SCOFFLAWS IN NEW YORK CITY
(most unpaid parking tickets to date)

1.	450 W. 38th Street Service Corp., Manhattan	$10,640
2.	Bear Building Corp., Bklyn	$ 7,828
3.	Gerald Gonzales, Bklyn	$ 6,705
4.	Anthony Haynes, Bronx	$ 6,700
5.	Susan Morales, Queens	$ 6,384
6.	Road Runners Trucking, Manhattan	$ 6,338

7. Arlene Jennings, Queens $ 5,852
8. Uniformed Fire Officers Assn. $ 5,090
9. Dale Francis, Bklyn $ 5,087
10. Paul Henry, Queens $ 4,644

REVENUES FROM PARKING TICKETS	
'91	286 million
'92	276 million
'93	255 million
'94	250 million
'95	290 million
'96 (projected)	346 million

Source: Dept. of Finance

OTHER CITY GARAGES WHERE YOUR CAR MAY BE IMPOUNDED

Besides Pier 76 -- Here is a list of other city garages on where your car might have wound up.

MANHATTAN

Pier 60: 12th Avenue & 19th Street,   971-0770

Washington Hgts: W 203rd St. & 9th Ave,   569-9099

BRONX

Mott Haven: 745 East 141st St. (Bruckner Blvd.)
                                 718-585-0821

QUEENS

Maspeth: 56th Rd & Laurel Hill Blvd.

718-786-7140

Whitestone: Linden Place & Whitestone Expwy

718-445-0100

Jamaica: 92-33 168th St. (Jamaica Ave.)

718-658-5182

BKLYN

Ft. Greene: Bklyn Navy Yard, Sand & Navy Sts.

718-834-1151

NEW YORK FUN FACT

Don't feel too bad if your car eventually gets the hook. According to then mayoral candidate, Rudolph Giuliani, speaking at a press conference at the Sheraton Centre, all of the following vehicles have been towed by the Department of Transportation:

TOW CASUALTIES IN NEW YORK CITY

- Drug enforcement cars while making a bust
- An FBI car
- A New York City Police car

There are over 30 different city agencies that can issue parking tickets. According to some sources, traffic enforcement agents have a quota of writing at least 100 tickets daily.

New York City's Secret Weapon...
The Blue Zone

A blue zone is a commercial area (mostly on narrow streets) in lower Manhattan that's restricted to parking Monday-Friday from 7 am-7 p.m. The area runs as far north as Frankfort and Dover Streets to the southern tip of Manhattan Island. It also extends to South Street on the East Side and as far west as State Street. A blue line is *supposed* to help determine an area in question which runs parallel to the curb. A blue sign is also suppose to identify the area as such. But don't bet on it. This one is the city's secret weapon.

Areas like the South Street Seaport and Wall Street fall into this category and in a good many cases, blue zone warning signs are obstructed, hidden or worse yet completely missing. Just when you think you've lucked out and found a space, you car may be towed. Beware. Sometimes the parking lot is a better choice.

The thing to remember here is that the city doesn't need a sign to enforce this regulation. When questioned, Alan Fromberg, a spokesman for the Department of Transportation, defended the practice by saying "blue paint doesn't adhere to cobblestoned streets anyway."

THE URBAN
GUERRRILLA

In an effort to find a parking place, some unscrupulous motorists have actually gone to the trouble of getting film permits from the city for posting in their windshields. When in production, film and television crews are often exempt from parking restrictions on city streets.

TOP 10 NEW YORK TOWAWAY ZONES

Pct.	Area	Tows
18	Midtown North	24,211
84	Brooklyn Heights	14,961
13	Grammercy Park	10,607
10	Chelsea	9,159
20	Upper West Side	8,821
6	Greenwich Village, Soho	8,571
34	Washington Heights	5,686
17	East Side	5,317
1	Wall Street	4,386
14	Midtown South	3,704
	Citywide Total:	143,420

Areas With Least Amount of Towings: East Harlem, Harlem, Manhattan Valley, Upper Harlem, Spanish Harlem, Borough Park, Fort Hamilton, Bay Ridge, Lower East Side, and Bensonhurst.

Staten Island has the very least amount of cars towed.

Source: Dept. of Transportation, Fiscal Year July 1994 - Sept. 1995.

10 REASONS TO HAVE
A PARKING SUMMONS DISMISSED

Things to look out for on your new ticket:

Dates & Time Defects
① No "time or date" of "First Observance for Meter Feeding";
② Violation *date* missing, Violation *time* indication a.m. or p.m. missing;

Location Defects
③ No "In Front of" or "Opposite" address or site specific details given or location described as "Corner of";

Vehicle Specific Defects
④ Incorrect or Missing: license plate type or number; car make, body type, state registration number (NYS only out of state N/A);

Ticket Specific Defects
⑤ No a.m. or p.m. *from regulation sign* listed;
⑥ "NO" Parking Standing, Stopping stated;
⑦ Days and hours of restriction not listed;
⑧ No meter serial number;
⑨ No feet measurement from hydrant (15' from both sides minimum);
⑩ No "All" box not checked or "Anytime" not stated (for NO Parking Standing, Stopping).

Source: Louis Camporeale, legal researcher and creator of
Parking Pal

KEY NUMBERS

- *Parking Information*   718-361-8000

- *Traffic Enforcement Agy,*
  (to get a double-parker ticketed)   212-996-8584

- *24-hr. Towed/vehicle info*   212-869-2929

- *Police Dept. Tow Operations*   212-262-4301

New Year NYC Parking Rule Suspensions 1997
(call 442-7080 just to be sure)
Holiday dates change from year to year

Jan 1	New Years Day	Legal Holiday
Jan 15	Martin Luther King's Birthday	No sweeping
Feb. 8-10	Eid al-Fitr	No sweeping
Feb. 12	Lincoln's Birthday	No sweeping
Feb. 17	Washington's Birthday (observed)	No sweeping
Mar 27	Holy Thursday	No sweeping
Mar 28	Good Friday	No sweeping
Apr 17-19	Eid al-Adha	No sweeping
Apr 21-22	Passover	No sweeping
Apr 24	Holy Thursday (Orthodox)	No sweeping
Apr 25	Good Friday (Orthodox)	No sweeping
Apr 28-29	Passover (7th-8th day)	No sweeping
May 8	Solemnity of Ascension	No sweeping
May 26	Memorial Day (observed)	Memorial Day
June 11	Shabuoth (1st Day)	No sweeping
June 12	Shabuoth/second day	No sweeping

Jul 4	Independence Day	Legal Holiday
Aug 15	Assumption of Blessed Virgin	No sweeping
Sep 1	Labor Day	Legal Holidays
Oct 2	Rosh Hashanah	No sweeping
Oct 3	Rosh Hashanah (2nd Day)	No sweeping
Oct 11	Yom Kippur	No sweeping
Oct 13	Columbus Day (Observed)	Legal Holiday
Oct 16	Succoth (1st day)	No sweeping
Oct 17	Succoth (2nd Day)	No sweeping
Oct 23	Shemini Atzereth	No sweeping
Oct 24	Simchas Torah	No sweeping
Nov 1	All Saints Day	No sweeping
Nov 4	Election Day	No sweeping
Nov 11	Veteran's Day	No sweeping
Nov 27	Thanksgiving Day	Legal Holiday
Dec 8	Immaculate Conception	No sweeping
Dec 25	Christmas Day	Legal Holiday

(The *Parking Pal* Sun Visor and Primer - a highly colorful calendar that highlights parking rules and street cleaning suspensions throughout the year - contains other useful features including parking signs in special communities throughout all boroughs, send $3.95 + 1.00 shipping to Parking Pal, PO Box 350-003, Bklyn, NY 11235)

Parking Violations Help Centers

Bronx	1400 Williamsbridge Rd. Brx, 10461	447-4430
Bklyn	210 Joralemon St. Bklyn, 11201	447-4430
Manh	1 Centre St. NYC, 10007	447-4430
Queens	89-61 162nd St. Jamaica, 11433	447-4430
Stat Isl	350 St. Marks Pl. Staten Isl, 10301	447-4430

- **IF THE PVB HOTLINE IS COLD CALL THE COMMISSIONER'S OFFICE AT 669-4855.**

MORE NEW YORK FUN FACTS

- The PVB issued a whopping 9.9 million tickets from July 1, 1994 through June 30, 1995.

- Since 1994 -- 40,000 tickets have been dismissed because they were improperly written.

- In 1995, more than 130 traffic enforcement officers had been assaulted. The Mayor's office has now made these city employees part of the Police Department in the hope of discouraging future assaults.

Foreign Diplomats and Parking Tickets

Foreign Embassies that lead the way in summonses - (which they routinely ignore!)

Russia	24,467	Ukraine	3,479
Indonesia	8,909	Egypt	3,428
Nigeria	5,657	Brazil	3,361
Bulgaria	4,609	Iran	2,224
Israel	3,853	Malaysia	2,180

Source: Dept. Of Finance 1995

#18

INVASION OF THE CHINESE TAKE-OUT MENUS

You haven't experienced New York City to the fullest until you've had every imaginable Chinese take-out menu dumped in your lobby, forcibly stuffed in your mailbox, or shoved under your door.

A good many of us have come home, only to find our floors littered with a plethora of take-out menus. Menus that we've had the misfortune to slip and slide upon on our way in. We pick them up, throw out our backs, only to find another collection waiting for us when we return.

You've tried putting up signs warning delivery people to desist, but to no avail. You might have delivered your own angry message to the owner and manager who authorizes such dumpings and they agree to stop, but guess what? The menus still keep on coming.

"I wrote the restaurant and told them I'm going to accumulate the menus you're dumping in my lobby and take you to court," said West Sider Saul Lapidus. The menus continued to pour in. "The judge ruled that leaving menus on private property was a violation of the first amendment, besides trespassing and littering." Mr. Lapidus won a settlement of $440 in his judgment against the Empire Szechuan restaurant.

Mr. Lapidus said in a recent interview that Chinese take-out menus are hazardous to your health because;

- ☹ The more menus that remain uncollected, the more they indicate that that no one is home, and that invites crime.
- ☹ Building owners are often fined by the Department of Sanitation for not cleaning the menus in front of their property.
- ☹ It's a waste of paper and bad for the environment.
- ☹ You sometimes can slip on menus in the lobby, particularly when they're on waxed or marble floors.

Yet for all the complaints that have been voiced against restaurant owners, in most cases the menus just keep on coming. There are those restaurateurs who admit that it pays to keep distributing menus because take-out is a significant part of their business. Many tenants continue to order from the menus and don't place this nuisance high on their list of priorities. "I can live with a few menus under my door," said Jeffrey Archer, a tenant on the West Side. "This doesn't affect my health the way crime and noise does."

GET A GRIP

- If you want to stop the influx of misguided menus from winding up in your apartment and you're up a great wall wondering what your next step should be, consider getting in touch with the CPOP division of your local police precinct.

- CPOP (the acronym stands for *Community Police Officer Program*) is made up of police officers who are assigned to very specific sections of your neighborhood. Call your local precinct to find out which officers are designated to your street.

- CPOP officers' responsibilities include dealing with merchants and local problems. What should follow your complaint is a warning to the restaurant, then very possibly a littering summons against the establishment.

According to Council Member Ronnie Eldridge's office, there have been documented instances such as that of Empire Szechuan on Broadway and 97th Street when establishments in the city have been denied use of an outdoor cafe as a result of their failure to abide by local community boards. The Empire chain of restaurants has been cited as the leading menu dumper throughout Manhattan.

Talk show host Dick Cavett shared his own method for getting even by "Collecting all the menus in my lobby and dropping them out of a fighter jet at 10,000 feet over Mei Ling Gardens."

Being bombarded on a daily basis with these take-out menus is another ritual the New Yorker has learned to endure. This practice not only puts illegal aliens to work, but helps defoliate our rainforests needed to make the menus, and brings advertising onto private property.

If you've ever wondered how the Chinese menu guys gain access to your building, remember that anyone can be buzzed into your lobby by identifying themselves as U.P.S.

THE INSIDE SCOOP ON MSG

When dining at the Chinese restaurant of your choice, chances are very good that the commonly used food enhancer, MSG (Monosodium Glutamate), which causes headaches, flushing, and mouth numbness in those susceptible, *remains* in your appetizer or soup despite whatever the waiter assures you.

These items are usually prepared in advance and are not made fresh to order. The waiter might suggest otherwise, but odds are it's *still* in your food. Inside sources tell you to keep this in mind next time you feel like wolfing down your next Pu Pu Platter.

Get-A-Grip: Eat only made to order dishes.

THE URBAN
GUERRILLA

Publisher Philip Seldon knows of one individual who took a group of homeless people out to dinner at a restaurant that qualified as one of the worst menu offenders. The individual made sure that the raunchiest individuals possible were hand picked.

Once he was seated with his guests, patrons high tailed it out from the stench alone. It would be safe to presume that the restaurant remembered this night for months to come. According to the individual who shall remain nameless, it's all perfectly legal and the management of a restaurant cannot refuse to serve his guests without violating discrimination laws.

(Another variation of this ploy is just to sit at a table with a group of friends and not order a thing.)

Some irate citizens have been known to try other tactics in order to get the restaurant's attention if their budget doesn't allow for the above mentioned. A resident known simply as "T.R." admitted to having taken several huge bags of garbage and parking them directly in front of the restaurant in question just prior to when the Department of Sanitation inspectors make their weekly rounds.

Of course this is not recommended by law abiding citizens but I'm told one can easily find out when these inspections occur simply by calling the DOS and following up. The offending restaurant should qualify for a summons thanks to an anonymous effort.

Submitted for your approval on the following page, a sign intended for delivery people complete with warning in Chinese and English -- suitable for posting in your lobby.

NEW YORK FUN FACTS

Seems the anti-menu revolt was at its height in 1993, when a gang of irate citizens formed the *Menu Warriors.* The group gathered all their take-out menus, visited the offending restaurants at the dinner hour, and tore them up in front of their customers.

Writer Phil Carlo of the Upper West Side once broke the jaw of a delivery guy who wouldn't stop distributing menus in his building. He spent 60 days on Rikers Island.

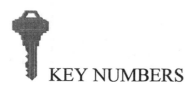

KEY NUMBERS

- *Sanitation Enforcement*   718-714-2730

- *DOS Commissioner's office*   212-788-4125

- *Menu Warriors*   787-6224
Join a group of equally irate menu receivers
by visiting the Chinese restaurant of choice and
tearing up their take-out menus *en masse* at dinner hour

RECENT DEVELOPMENTS

In an effort to prevent menu and flyer dumping on private property, Assemblyman Scott Stringer has introduced legislation (A. 2240) that would make the owner and managers of restaurants (as well as other commercial establishments) responsible for each menu bearing its name. The fines would be increased from $50-$250 to $1,000. All in all, that's a lot of Lo Mein.

The bill is intended to make businesses more responsive to community concerns. As the Assemblyman puts it, "The quality of day-to-day life of the average New Yorker should not be disregarded in their own home."

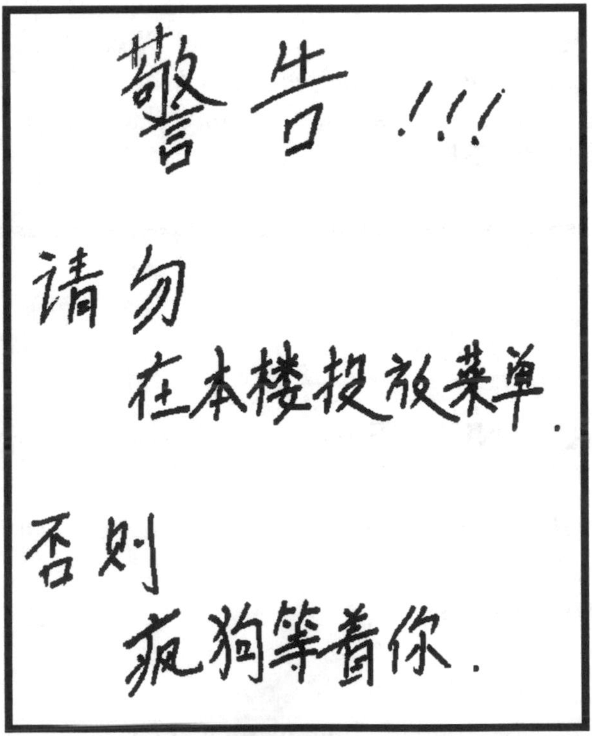

警告！！！

请勿
在本楼投放菜单．

否则
疯狗等着你．

**Please don't put any menus here otherwise
the crazy dog will be waiting for you!**

#19

KAMIKAZE ROLLERBLADERS
SOCIOPATHIC SKATEBOARDERS

Up to now the physiological effects associated with living in New York have been limited to hearing loss, high blood pressure and respiratory illness. Throw in the disco across the street and the super's dog that humps your leg every other Thursday and you get a good picture what you're up against.

Just when you think you've got one preventable irritant under control another one quickly takes its place. This time it's in the form of rollerbladers and skateboarders who have as much concern for public safety as a blowtorch.

Presently there are 500,000 in-line skaters in New York. The Central Park Medical Unit estimates that 900 to 1,000 skaters a year are injured and require some form of hospitalization. Nationally, 42 skaters have been killed in accidents since January 1992. 9 of which occurred in New York - the most of any state in the nation according to the US Consumers Product Safety Commission Most deaths have been caused by skaters who have collided with autos or lost their balance. In 1995, it has been estimated that as many as 105,000 of in-line skaters had injuries that called for emergency room treatment.

GET A GRIP

- To begin with, the law states that anyone younger than 14 years of age must wear a helmet when rollerblading in the city. However, those who are reckless or not observing traffic regulations are subject to fines up to $100 thanks to the new Local Law # 43 - Section 19-176.1 of the Administrative Code.

- The law specifically prohibits "reckless operation." This term is defined as endangering the safety or property of another and is punishable in accordance with section 1800 of the vehicle and traffic law. Penalties are not less than $50 and not more than $100. In January of 1996, New York became the first state to pass a law regulating in-line skating.

A ban on outlawing skaters from city sidewalks was defeated by the City Council as being a bit too stringent for New Yorkers. As they say at Shea Stadium, "wait until next year."

ROLLERCOPS ON THE LOOSE

Park Rangers on in-line skates have now taken to the roadways in Central Park all in an effort to nab reckless rollerbladers.

- New York City now joins the ranks of Ft. Lauderdale and Montreal as one of the places that employs Rollercops who instruct skaters, bicyclists and joggers not to go against traffic. They also distribute rule books and safety guides.

- Rollercops can issue a summons but they don't carry any weapons.

NEW YORK NOT-SO-FUN FACT

According to the Central Park Medical Unit -- of the 1,000 injuries in a year, 40% involve in line skaters.

THE URBAN GUERRILLA

Senior citizens have the home advantage on this gripe.
I always advocate sticking out your cane if you have one when the next kamikaze comes speeding along.

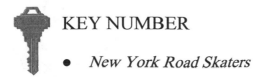

KEY NUMBER

- *New York Road Skaters*   534-7858

#20

TWO WHEEL TERRORS

Brace yourselves for reckless bicyclists with little or no regard for public safety. Every year in New York City hundreds of people get injured (in some cases killed) in accidents with crazed bicyclists, who in turn often get injured by motorists. Nationwide it is estimated that 1,000 a year die while riding bikes.

GET A GRIP

- Section 19-176 of the NYC Administrative Code now gives the police the authority to *seize* and *confiscate* any bicycle on the spot from a reckless cyclist. *Note: On the down side, this provision can't be enforced until the city Environmental Control Board issues regulations and guidelines on how the bikes may be seized. So stay tuned for new developments.*

- The speed limit for bicycles has been established at 35 MPH.

- Currently in the City Council is additional legislation (Intro.577) calling for bike messengers to be licensed with the City of New York and to possess a minimum amount of liability insurance. This bill would also require commercial delivery cyclists who fail to carry identification, as required under existing law, to be penalized anywhere from $25 to $250.

- In the meantime, do write the Speaker of City Hall, Peter Vallone, and the Chairperson of the Transportation Committee, Noach Dear, (see end of chapter) telling them that you favor strong legislation protecting pedestrians from the infamous "*spokes-people.*"

- By not complaining, the message you are sending is that everything's all right. These days, that seems to be the last thing most of us want to convey to legislators.

NYS Vehicle and Traffic Law (section # 1231) requires bicyclists to be bound by the same laws as motorists *(Honk once if you've ever seen a bicyclist issued a ticket for running a red light.)* This one is about as hard to get enforced as an anti-urinating ordinance in Central Park. Nevertheless, bikers must obey all traffic signs, signals, stop signs, red lights, ride in the correct direction of a one way street, and in traffic, cyclists should ride on the far right.

With administrations and priorities changing, we are now lucky to have 2,000 citations handed out annually, not to mention enforcement.

Should an accident occur, commercial establishments employing bikers (as well as the pedal pusher) are to be held liable, according to section 10-157 of the City Administrative Code. Commercial bikers must identify their employers by way of a sign on the rear of the bicycle or attached to the delivery basket. That ID must include name, address, and phone number. Bikers are now required to carry personal identification (name, address, photo) as well as company ID.

Businesses that make bike deliveries must keep a log book. The book must contain the following with regard to each delivery biker:
- name
- residential address
- date of employment
- identification number
- destination

Whether they're messengers or fast food jockeys, their employers are responsible for their riding habits. The harsh reality is that the summons invariably gets ignored not only by the merchant, but by the police as well.

<u>Drop a short note to:</u>

✓ Noach Dear Councilmember
Chairperson of Transportation Committee
4620 18th Avenue
Brooklyn, NY 11204

✓ Speaker Peter Vallone
City Hall
New York, NY 10007

I recently heard of one New Yorker who witnessed a rollerblader colliding head-on into a bicyclist (neither one was hurt just shaken up.) "Isn't that something," said the onlooker. "I guess I should feel bad...." he said shaking his head. "But I have to admit I don't."

It's The Law!

Section 4-07 (3) of the *Rules of New York City* (available at the Municipal Library - 31 Chambers St.) makes it illegal to ride on the sidewalk. The law clearly states that "No person shall ride or operate a bicycle upon any sidewalk area unless permitted by sign". Children under 12 years of age riding wheels less than 26 inches in diameter are exempt.

NEW YORK FUN FACT

In 1988-89 nearly 20,000 summonses got handed out by the police department to reckless cyclists. A NYPD task force tried to tackle the problem. Since then, the force was eliminated, due mostly to office fax machines replacing bike messengers.

KEY NUMBERS

- *Department of Transportation*   442-7852

- *S.T.O.P.* Stop Traffic Offenses Program.
Motor vehicle lawlessness, anti-bicycle movement 935-0990

- *Walk New York*   718-855-7134

- *Transportation Alternatives*   475-4600

- *Pedestrians First*
contact Bette Deuing
c/o *Our Town*
242 W. 30th Street, NYC, 10001   268-8600

#21

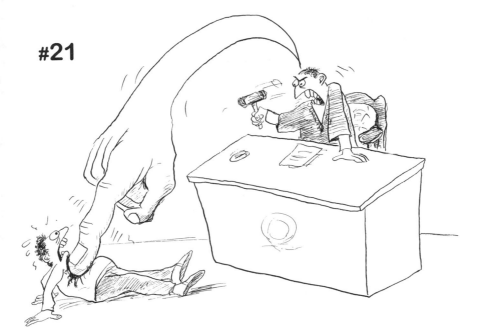

THE WHOLE TRUTH ABOUT SURVIVING SMALL CLAIMS COURT

You've tried contacting the guy who won't pay up. You've called and written only to find that he's either 'away from his desk' or 'tied up in an important meeting.' Perhaps he can't come to the phone or worse yet he's suddenly on vacation. The excuses are endless.

What might possibly be the next step is taking the scoundrel to Small Claims Court, also referred to as "The People's Court," where according to Chief Clerk Jack Baer, over 100 cases are heard on any given night in Manhattan alone. Small Claims court enables a person to file a claim without the use of a lawyer for financial reimbursement up to

$3,000 in New York. New Jersey on the other hand only allowed until recently compensation for up to $1000, while Virginia and Tennessee allow one to sue for as much as $10,000.

Personally I've been through the process myself 5 times, (*and won all 5 settlements*) but as Senior Court Clerk Joe Gebbia says, "you have to make sure that you know who you're suing." Suing the wrong party or name is one of the biggest mistakes one can make." If on the other hand, you come prepared, keep accurate records, and are concise, you have a very good chance of prevailing.

THE NITTY GRITTY DETAILS

Time-Saving Tips

If you do decide that your day is in court, I recommend doing *all* of the following:

☛ Make sure to sue the **legal name** of the individual or business. If you do sue improperly, even though the judgment may be in your favor, it will be worthless in terms of enforcement. Without fail, many people unwittingly commit this error.

☛ Check the business certificate of either the individual or company by way of the County Clerk's office, Department of Consumer Affairs, Secretary of State (in Albany at 518-474-6200) or Better Business Bureau *(see Survival chapter).* A company must post their New York State license in full view.

☛ Go directly to the County Clerk's office (in Manhattan: Supreme Court Bldg., 60 Centre street, basement - room 117B - Examination of Certificates.) Look up the business in one of its alphabetized directories. Be sure you are suing the proper legal name by looking carefully at the certificate for identifying names and making a copy of it for your records.

☛ You then can file a claim at Small Claims Court in any of the counties (see end of this chapter). Manhattan Small Claims is at 111 Centre Street, room 323, from 9 a.m. to 4:30 PM, Mon.-Fri. You'll have to pay a five dollar filing fee that is reimbursed if you win the judgment.

☛ Make sure that the defendant has a NYC address. You must sue in the correct county. For example: you live in Manhattan but the defendant has his business in Nassau county, you must then file your claim in Nassau county - - and so on.

☛ When you do file with Small Claims, you will be asked to fill out a description of what has transpired. Be as precise as possible and make sure you can back it all up with evidence. You will then be given a day in court, usually in 4-6 weeks time.

☛ Prior to court, be prepared. Bring receipts, contracts, letters, estimates, photographs, and witnesses if necessary. You get one shot so make it count!

☛ On the day that your hearing is scheduled your name will be called on the calendar. You should be aware that if you chose to go 'by the court' that the judge only gets to hear about 2-3 cases a night. It is for certain that this will involve months of return visits because of back-logged cases. True, you have the right to appeal by having the judge hear your case, but it will prove both time-consuming and very costly.

☞ Your hearing will be facilitated by choosing an arbitrator who is a volunteer attorney. After a judgment is rendered it will be mailed to you in the next several weeks. An arbitrator's decision *may not* be appealed.

Attorney Steven Shapiro, who has been serving as an arbitrator in Small Claims for the past five years, states that 85% of the cases in Small Claims are heard by arbitrators who use the same standards and apply the same law.

COLLECTING YOUR JUDGMENT

"If the case goes to trial, the collection rate is about 74%," says Mr. Gebbia. "Which puts it right up there with supreme court and civil court." This, according to an independent survey conducted several years ago. If the case goes to default (where one party doesn't show up), the collection rate drops down to 41%. Mr. Gebbia, who's been working as a supervisor in Small Claims for 26 years, says that by far the biggest mistake committed by those filing a judgment is suing the wrong party. Mr. Baer adds, "In a lot of cases if somebody doesn't have assets, you're stuck."

KEY STEPS TO TAKE TO INSURE COLLECTION:

☞ If the defendant has not honored the judgment you must locate their assets. If you *don't* know where the defendant's assets are kept, you will then have to go back to where you filed your claim and take out an *Information Subpoena,* which costs $2. The subpoena is used to help locate the defendant's bank account. Your next hope is that its kept under the same name as stated in your judgment.

☞ Serve the subpoena to a company or individual that the defendant does business with. It is imperative that you find out what bank the defendant does business with. If you have paid by check, just turn it over and see where it has been deposited.

☞ Serve the legal department of either Nynex or Con Edison. Utility companies may consider your request "low priority." Be prepared to pursue them if they don't honor your request in a reasonable period of time. Also consider landlords and cable companies as good sources.

☞ Once you have located their assets, take out a restraining notice that will "freeze" their account. Next, bring that information to the Sheriff's office. It is here that the Deputy Sheriff has the authority to go into the defendant's bank account and retrieve your settlement. The filing fee for this procedure is $30 and it is reimbursable should you finally collect.

☞ The Marshall or Sheriff can seize and sell assets and turn over the proceeds to you. Employers and banks may be served for salary and asset garnishment until a debt is cleared.

☞ If your judgment involved the operation of a motor vehicle and hasn't been paid for 45 days, you can have his or her driver's license or auto registration suspended. Forms are available at the Small Claims Court clerk's office.

GET A GRIP

- Choose an arbitrator. Your case will be heard faster. Arbitrators apply the same law as the judge but without the right to appeal.

- Come to court prepared. Bring canceled checks, repair bills, agreements, photographs, even a witness who will testify on your behalf. Be concise.

- Know what you're going to say ahead of time and don't come on *too* strongly with either the arbitrator or the judge so as to put them off. Being argumentative can work against you.

- Don't get discouraged that the system is slow. Don't hold municipal employees to your time table.

- For future reference, never pay in cash! Always pay by check. That way you can see where your money is deposited and more importantly, where they keep their assets.

- "Above all," as Mark Twain once said, "when in doubt, tell the truth...it's easier to remember."

NEW YORK FUN FACT

The county that has the most small claims activity
is Queens.
Most commercial cases are heard in Manhattan.
Most Landlord-Tenant cases are heard in the Bronx.

KEY NUMBERS

- *Small Claims Court*   374-5776

- *Ass't Commissioner Private Sector*
  of the Sheriff's office   240-6700

- *Small Claim Support Line*   349-6460
  (Don't get mad, get even,
  will refer you to a local Action Center
  phone number where they will answer
  questions about filing a claim.)

- *NY Bar Association Referral Line*   626-7373

Outer Borough Small Claims Courts

Queens   120-55 Queens Blvd.   718-520-3633
                Kew Gardens, NY 11424

Brooklyn   141 Livingston St.   718-643-7913
                Bklyn, NY 11201   718-643-7914

Staten Isl.   927 Carleton Ave   718-390-5421
                Staten Island, NY 10310

Bronx   851 Grand Concourse   718-590-3568
                Bronx, NY 10451

- Note...Each of the civil courts in the five NYC boroughs has a 'pro se attorney' on staff who can provide a free legal consultation. All you have to do is locate them.

SOME ALTERNATIVES TO SMALL CLAIMS

A. Compromise... Consider settling for half of what's owed you unless you feel you want to drive the point home. Then be prepared for a time commitment once you get to court.

B. Mission Letter...Write a letter setting a date aside when you expect to hear from the party in question. Be firm in stating your expectations and make it clear that other alternatives will then be utilized.

C. Mediate...Contact the mediation center in your borough and meet with a trained mediator. They will help negotiate a fair settlement. All options should be explored before proceeding to court.

FEE STRUCTURES

When filing a claim, remember to bring exact change. If you don't -- you'll have to lose your place, get change somewhere, and return to the back of the line.

Small Claim	$ 5.84
2 Small Claims	11.68
3 Small Claims	17.52

If you're a corporation, partnership or association, you'll need to file a Commercial Claim $ 22.84
  2 Commercial Claims   45.68

  Transcript of judgment $ 15.00

If you're over 65 or disabled your case can be heard in the daytime.

#22

"Since I got laid off by the post office
I'm feeling a little -- disgruntled."
Rocko's Modern Life

IS THIS HELL...
OR ARE WE *JUST* AT THE
POST OFFICE ?

The term, "Postal Service" seems to be another one of those wacky oxymorons New Yorkers have learned to endure. I'll grant you that New Yorkers are a hearty bunch, they're infinitely more resilient than any other creature on the face of the planet. They have to be. The average New Yorker would have made an excellent Viking. Just give him his trusty shield and a good pair of running shoes to dodge anything this great city throws his way and watch him dance. In this case, the odds are overwhelming that he'll be faced with not only a long line at the neighborhood post office but an exceedingly slow one at that. To top things off he'll be dealing with government workers who just don't give a flying fizzle and looks that could kill. All this despite postage rates that have risen 11 times since 1971. But in all fairness, the US postage stamp remains one of the least expensive in the world. Try comparing it to Japan and Germany's postal rates. First class postage in both countries is about 70 cents, more than double our rate.

If you've waited on line you know how frustrating an experience it can be to deal with civil service employees. Many of us have wanted to light one huge bonfire under their collective behinds. Do you think for a moment that they'd be moving at the same geriatric pace if suddenly they were put on commission? Until such wishes are granted, take it from some folks who watch their blood pressure:

☞ *Always* bring along something to read, or listen to your personal stereo/cassette player while on line. Instead of getting annoyed that the line isn't moving as fast as you'd like it to, be sure to allow yourself at least thirty to forty-five minutes in scheduling.

☞ *Don't* go to the post office at peak hours which fall between 1 p.m. and 3 p.m. For other days and times see the end of this chapter.

To start off with it helps to be somewhat courteous, leaving behind the notion that you're on enemy territory. Municipal employees are used to being on the receiving end of daily complaints and dealing with some very bizarre individuals, especially in New York.

☞ Post Office personnel are most likely to work with you if you project a pleasant attitude and ask them for their help.

GET A GRIP

- Use the time that you are standing on line creatively by either writing down some thoughts, reading, day dreaming, or listening to your cassette player. As a psychologist friend of mine suggested, take the urgency and stress out of your wait by taking a short mental vacation. You'll do wonders for your blood pressure and deal with this mother of all aggravations in a positive way.

- If, on the other hand, you feel things are getting out of control, fill out a postal service consumer card at your branch and state your complaint. From personal experience, the Postmaster's office will usually follow up with you in a week's time. Consider contacting the new US Postal Consumer Affairs Office - see *Key Numbers* at the end of chapter.

THE NEW POSTAL ADVISORY COUNCIL

Some post offices in New York City have set up a new operation known as the *Local Customer Advisory Council,* which is part of the Community Action Council. The Council allows customers, local politicians as well as the post office, the opportunity to sit down about once a month, and work with the community directly on local problems. They will listen to your frustrations, problems, and horror stories. Because it is a relatively new feature, not all NYC branches are set up for this operation.

The Council is set up at branches where there is consistent residential and business traffic. Residents will now have direct input in resolving issues related to any postal complaint. If you want to blow off some steam, it may be worth your while to get in touch with the station manager at your branch. Find out when the next meeting is scheduled. It might be worth a shot -- instead of having your gripe fall on deaf ears.

WORST TIMES TO GO TO THE POST OFFICE IN NYC

- THE DAY AFTER ANY HOLIDAY
- THE FIRST OF THE MONTH
- LAST DAY OF THE MONTH
- 1-3 PM*
- RIGHT AFTER WORK. USUALLY 5-6 PM

*Generally this is when the shifts change and postal employees go to lunch. Most post offices are short staffed. Service is slower than usual.

Source: U.S. Postal Clerks

BEST OF THE WORST TIMES....(USUALLY)

Pick 'em. Generally, first thing in the morning, 9-11 am hours or one hour before closing.

BEST REASON <u>NOT</u> TO USE POST OFFICE VENDING MACHINES....

They give out Susan B. Anthony dollars as change.

KEY NUMBERS

- *P.O. Consumer Affairs Office*   330-3668
  421 Eighth Av., Rm. 4202-0 NY, NY 10199

- *Postmaster's office*   330-3602

- *Zip Code Information*   967-8585

- *Mail Fraud, Theft, Obscene*   330-3844

- *Post Office Answer Line*   330-4000

MANHATTAN POST OFFICE BRANCHES

* Main Post Office:		
8th Ave & 33rd St.	*10001*	330-2908
* Ansonia:		
40 West 66th St	*10023*	362-7486
Audubon:		
511 W 165th St.	*10032*	568-3311
Bowling Green:		
25 Broadway	*10004*	363-9490
Bryant:		
23 W 43rd St.	*10036*	279-5960
Canal Street:		
350 Canal St.	*10013*	925-3378
Cathedral:		
215 W 104th St.	*10025*	662-9191
Cherokee:		
1539 First Ave.	*10028*	288-3724
Chinatown:		
6 Doyers St.	*10013*	267-3510
Church Street:		
90 Church St.	*10007*	330-5247
College:		
217 W 140th St.	*10030*	283-2235
Colonial Park:		
99 Macombs Pl	*10039*	368-4211

Columbia Univ:
1123 Amst'dam Av	*10025*	864-1874

Columbus Circle:
27 W 60th St.	*10023*	265-7858

* Cooper:
93 Fourth Ave	*10003*	254-1389

Empire State:
19 W 33rd St.	*10001*	736-8282

Fort George:
4558 Broadway	*10040*	942-0052

Fort Washington:
3771 Broadway	*10032*	368-7302

* FDR:
909 Third Ave	*10022*	330-5549

Governors Island:
Bldg. 140	*10004*	943-9696

Gracie Station:
229 E 85th St.	*10028*	988-6681

Grand Central:
Lex. Ave - 45th St.	*10017*	826-4677

Greeley Square:
40 W 32nd St.	*10001*	244-7055

Hamilton Grange:
521 W 146th St.	*10031*	281-8401

Hell Gate:
153 E 110th St.	*10029*	860-3557

Inwood:
90 Vermilyea St.	*10034*	567-3032

Island Station :
694 Island Main St.	*10044*	752-5564

Knickerbocker:
128 E Broadway	*10002*	227-0089

Lenox Hill:
217 E 70th St.	*10021*	879-4401

Lincolnton:
2266 Fifth Ave   10037   281-9781
London Terrace:
234 Tenth Ave   10011   242-8248
Madison Square:
149 E 23rd St.   10010   673-3771
* Manhattanville:
365 W 125th St.   10027   662-1901
Midtown:
221 W 38th St.   10018   944-6597
Morgan:
341 9th Ave   10199   330-2475
Morningside:
232 W 116th St.   10026   864-6968
Murray Hill:
115 E 34th St.   10016   689-9127
Murray Hill   :
205 East 36th St.   10016   689-1124
Old Chelsea Sta:
217 W 18th St.   10011   675-2415
Park West:
693 Columbus Ave   10025   866-7322
Patchin:
70 W 10th St.   10011   475-2534
Peck Slip:
1-15 Peck Slip   10038   964-1055
Peter Stuyvesant:
432 E 14th St.   10009   677-2112
Pitt Station:
185 Clinton St.   10002   254-9270
Planetarium Sta:
127 W 83rd St.   10024   873-3701
Port Authority:
76 Ninth Ave   10011   929-9296
Prince:
103-05 Prince St.   10012   226-7868

Radio City:

322 W 52nd St.	*10019*	265-6677

Rockefeller Center:

610 Fifth Ave	*10020*	265-3854

Times Square:

340 W 42nd St.	*10036*	244-0111

Tompkins Square:

244 E 3rd St.	*10009*	673-6415

Triborough :

167 E 124th St.	*10035*	534-0865

Tudor:

5 Tudor City Pl.	*10017*	697-8656

United Nations:

42nd St.- First Ave	*10017*	754-7353

Village:

201 Varick Ave	*10014*	989-9741

Wall Street:

73 Pine St.	*10005*	269-2161

Washington Bridge:

555 W 180th St.	*10033*	568-7601

West Village:

527 Hudson St.	*10014*	989-5084

Yorkville:

1619 Third Ave	*10128*	369-2230

Station (# 138):

Macy's Bway/34th	*10001*	695-4400 ext. 2688

accepts passport applications

#23

(Cough, Gasp, Arrggghhh)

BUS AND TRUCK IDLING

Residents on Manhattan's Upper West Side were fuming mad about fumes. They didn't mind that bus loads of tourists and students were being dropped off at one such restaurant in their community. Crowds that made walking on the sidewalk difficult were also tolerable for the most part. But what the community couldn't accept was when bus drivers, who brought in the groups, allowed their engines to run indefinitely and spew out a sea of polluted fumes which affected their breathing.

Idling, as it is commonly referred to by the Department of Environmental Protection is illegal in New York City and carries with it a penalty of $450.00.

It happens mostly when drivers lean back in their seats and enjoy the benefits of air conditioning, heat and news on the hour by keeping their motor on. Commercial vehicles seem to be the most targeted for this violation and remains the main focus by the DEP's 30 citywide inspectors.

"When we catch someone doing this, a notice of violation goes to not only the bus driver for causing it, but the bus company for permitting it," said Jerry Ross, director of the air, noise and enforcement division at the Department of Environmental Protection. From 1994 through 1996 there were 1,395 summonses handed out to drivers by DEP inspectors for Idling. Ross states that prime areas for idling include the South Street Seaport, The Battery and the Theater District. "We step up our efforts in Spring and Summer because that's when the tourist season starts," said Ross.

Idling, involves diesel pollution and has been linked to asthma, bronchitis, emphysema and premature death, according to the Natural Resources Defense Council. The US Environmental Protection Agency states that at least 60,000 premature deaths occur each year by 'particle pollution' -- the type emitted by diesel buses.

When the driver leaves their engine running while the vehicle is in a stationary position for 3 or more minutes he is in violation of the law. Buses, delivery trucks, even the mayor's own chauffeur, can be found idling year round. What follows is polluted air filled with diesel soot and carbon monoxide floating around your pets, children, and everyone else vying for breathing room. Add that to the already polluted NYC air and the result can be deadly. Carbon monoxide creeps into your home via the windows and air ducts.

"Certain neighborhoods are more vulnerable to these type of annoyances because the bridge and tunnel crowd seems to frequent them more," says the DEP. "Bridge and Tunnel" is a term some New Yorkers are famous for using. It refers to those living in the outer boroughs who frequent Manhattan, particularly on the weekends.

GET A GRIP

- Idling is clearly a violation of New York City Law. The DEP recommends keeping a log of when "*Idlers*" are most likely to strike in your area. If you see a pattern being established, call the DEP at 718-DEP-HELP. A DEP inspector will be dispatched to your area.

- "It's always helpful for the caller to ask for an identification number" says Natalie Millner, a spokeswoman for the DEP. "That way if they call back their complaint will already be on file in the computer."

- As of July 1, 1996, any driver caught Idling by an Environmental Protection Investigator will be fined $500. To make matters even more memorable, the DEP -- at their sole discretion, can hit an Idler for the maximum fine which is $875 and can ticket the driver and company separately.

- Always remember to get the license plate number of the bus or truck that is idling along with their location. Bear in mind that refrigeration delivery trucks (ones that carry food), fire engines and ambulances are exempt from the law.

"The DEP presently receives more than 300,000 calls a year," says Millner of the DEP. Complaints take in water, sewer, air, noise and hazardous material.

It's the Law...Section 24-163 of NYC
Administrative Code states:

No person shall cause or permit the engine of a motor vehicle, other than a legally authorized emergency motor vehicle, to idle for longer than 3 minutes while parking as defined in section one hundred twenty-nine of the vehicle and traffic law, standing as defined in section one hundred forty five of the vehicle and traffic law, or stopping as defined in section one hundred forty seven of the vehicle and traffic law, unless the engine is used to operate a loading, unloading or processing device.

When the ambient temperature is in excess of forty degrees Fahrenheit, no person shall cause or permit the engine of a bus defined in section one hundred four of the vehicle and traffic law to idle while parking, standing, or stopping (as defined above) at any terminal point, whether or not enclosed, along an established route.

KEY NUMBER

- *Dept. of Environmental Protection*   **718-699-9811**

IF THIS HOTLINE PROVES TO BE COLD -- CALL...

- *Commissioner of DEP*   **718-595-6565**
- *Jerry Ross, Director of Enforcement*   **718-595-6579**

NEW YORK FUN FACT

Seems two inspectors spotted a bus near the Javits Convention Center that had been idling one afternoon. After timing the bus for the allotted time permitted, the inspectors approached the bus and to their amazement noticed it rocking back and forth. As they got nearer they watched as a hooker got off the bus. The affair turned out to be a little more expensive than the driver anticipated. He received a summons from the DEP.

#24

BUSES FROM HELL ...
AND WHY DO THEY COME
5 AT A TIME?

Has this ever happened to you? You're running late for an appointment. Perhaps you're going to work or to an engagement. The thought of taking a cab crosses your mind but wait -- here comes one of New York City's 3,600 buses right down the street. There isn't any traffic. You'll be there in no time and have a few bucks to spare. It seems simple enough. Only this is New York. Nothing is simple here. Most things wind up to be major productions. And today above all others is one you're not likely to forget. You've just stepped into the *Bus from Hell!*

NYC buses have progressively been losing riders according to a recent transportation survey,. Riders rated bus service in New York as slow, overcrowded and unreliable.

Not to mention requiring a lot of exact change. Buses also give off massive doses of diesel soot. That may explain why ridership on buses is down almost 50% over the past 30 years, according to a NYC Transportation Commissioner.

But more specifically, what exactly is the *bus from hell?* It occurs when the operator deliberately drives his bus with all the urgency of a constipated elephant running the Nairobi marathon. The driver intentionally catches every red light, stalls at bus stops, shoots the shit with other drivers, hardly has his foot on the accelerator, and makes "killing time" a required course at the bus academy.

Meanwhile, you're busy having your third in a series of panic attacks. At this point, crawling backwards on your stomach through the La Brea tar pits would have proven a faster mode of transportation. So why does this happen?

No brain surgeon needed here. As you probably guessed by now, the bus operator tries to keep on schedule or is ahead of schedule, aka *"running hot"* in the trade. Drivers are told by bus dispatchers at stops along the route to slow down. The operator also knows to do this at specific stops and times according to schedule.

Some in management believe it is more tolerable to be behind schedule than ahead of one. When the same condition occurs in a NYC subway, the train in the station is given *"holding lights."* This allows the train ahead to be considerably distanced and also limits your waiting time as a passenger -- in theory of course. The same rule of thumb applies to surface transit.

Drivers know whether they're behind schedule (aka *"running cold"*) by checking their arrival time at pre-determined stops along the way. If by chance they're *"running hot"*...bingo, a bus from hell is eagerly awaiting to be hatched from transit incubation.

BUNCHING IS NOT JUST FOR BANANAS

"Bunching" occurs when four and five buses, on the same route, come all at once causing large gaps in service for riders. "It is probably our largest complaint," says Kathy Severson, Manager of Customer Relations for the Department of Buses at New York City Transit.

The most common moment for such a convoy, contrary to widespread belief, is not when drivers decide to have their weekly poker game.   Rather it is when traffic and bus breakdowns outnumber passengers.

In actuality, the driver can call the route manager who would then help space out the buses along the route (don't hold your breath on this one either -- you have a better chance of getting struck by a bald-headed eagle in midtown). All too often the result is endless waiting at bus stops while nothing appears for 20 minutes. Suddenly a convoy of buses comes creeping over the horizon. Sound familiar? With new budget cuts, expect to wait longer at stations.

NEW YORK FUN FACT

Ever notice a strong acidic aroma at the exit doors of your favorite bus? Given a fairly hectic schedule, bus drivers very often urinate at this convenient spot when they're too lazy or unable to find a rest room. The more conscientious ones use a paper cup or perhaps a co-worker's thermos.

RECENT DEVELOPMENTS

As of late, an army of renegade privately owned mini-vans are cruising the city (Flatbush Avenue and Southeast Queens are the heart of mini-van country) and are having no trouble finding passengers. Seems the vans are far more efficient, accessible, quick, charge only a buck, and prove more attractive to commuters who are often fed up with city buses. The TA estimates a 20% loss in revenue along certain bus routes.

Other New Yorkers believe the greatest endorsement for taking a cab or subway is *still* a New York City bus.

GET A GRIP

- If you want to voice your complaint on any service problem concerning a NYC bus, (i.e. the bus never comes, rude operators, reckless driving, lack of ventilation, etc.) call *718-927-7499* at the Transit Authority. *If your complaint is about one of the city's 7,509 bus drivers, you must put it in writing.* Be sure to include the bus number (four digits found displayed inside, above where the driver sits, on the outside of the vehicle or on the back of the bus.) Also include the route number of the bus (i.e. M104, M27, etc.) and if you can get it, the driver's badge number. Also list the location of where the incident occurred and the date.

- "It is essential that we have as specific information as possible" says Severson. Most folks forget to write down any identifying numbers which is why a good many complaints fall short of any disciplinary action.

- Severson assures that your complaint will be taken quite seriously by the Customer Service Department of the Transit Authority. All queries will be acknowledged by reply. The driver will be brought in for a hearing. The incident will be followed up on and the driver will be reprimanded. In cases of multiple complaints, her or she may be suspended or in some cases dismissed. Ms. Severson went on to say that people who have been dismissed or suspended have had a history of complaints.

At last report, the Transit Authority has developed a secret new vehicle that will run at phenomenal speeds throughout the city and be exactly on time within one 1/1000th of a second. This vehicle is to be called the *Not In Service Bus.*

WORST BUS LINES IN NEW YORK

According to the NY Transit Authority the most often complained about bus routes in New York City based on bunching, slow service and notorious delays in traffic, rate as follows;

- ☠ M10
- ☠ M11
- ☠ M15
- ☠ M101
- ☠ M4
- ☠ B35 (Brooklyn)
- ☠ B41

- ☠ Q58 (Queens)
- ☠ Q43
- ☠ Bx12 (Bronx)
- ☠ Bx55
- ☠ S44 (Staten Island)

Source: MTA and Daily News survey

Most Common Complaints about New York City Buses:

① Bus Bunching
② Rude Operators
③ Reckless Driving
④ Boarding complaints *(closing the doors, not getting close to the curb, etc.)*
⑤ Fare Disputes *(refunds, Metrocard, etc.)*

KEY NUMBERS

Bus Complaints
● *Bus Customers Relations Center*   718-927-7499
25 Jamaica Avenue
Room 1
Brooklyn, NY 11207

Subway Complaints
● *MTA Customer Service,*   718-330-3322
Room 875
NYCTA
370 Jay Street
Brooklyn, NY 11201

● *MTA Inspector General's office*
(hazardous conditions, fraud, abuse)   800-MTA-4448
● *Straphangers Campaign*   349-6460
● *Private Bus Lines* (NY Franchise Bureau)   669-4500
                                                      442-8040

WHY DO THOSE *%$! SUBWAY TRAINS STOP IN THE MIDDLE OF THE PLATFORM WHILE I'M WAITING AT THE FAR END?

You stand at the furthermost end of the platform hoping to get a seat, possibly in the first car. The train finally arrives and stops short in the middle of the platform. Suddenly it's a mad dash to the train hoping the doors won't close before you get there. Is the motorman in need of a new pair of bi-focals or is he just plain sadistic?

This procedure happens mostly at non-rush hours or late at night - usually after 8:30 PM according to the TA. Seems the Transit Authority wants passengers to stand closer to the token booth or at designated areas which are usually distinguished by a yellow sign suspended from the ceiling. Reason being, then you're still in view of the token booth clerk who has a phone to call police and emergency medical service if need be.

For the world's most extensive subway, consisting of 722 miles of track and 137 miles of subway tunnels, this is a crime preventing measure. Actually, using the 'off hours' part of the platform will prevent you from tearing ass in your wingtips at the last moment.

With new budget cuts, the TA also operates with shorter trains at off peak hours.

New York City Transit Police Bureau Offices

- 59th St. & Columbus Circle IND A Line   586-6832
- 14th St. & Union Sq. BMT N-R Lines   254-4459
- Erickson Place & W. B'way IND A Line   226-4318
- 145th St. & St. Nicholas Av. IND A   368-9609

TOP 10 MOST DANGEROUS & DECREPIT SUBWAY STATIONS IN THE CITY

10. Second Avenue   F Line
 9. Bowery   J, M
 8. Canal Street   J, M, 2, N, R, 6
 7. Franklin Ave   S
 6. Botanical Garden S
 5. Beach 98th St.   A
 4. Sutter Ave   L
 3. Livonia Ave   L
 2. 110th St.   2, 3
 1. E. Tremont Ave   2, 5

Source: Dean Chang - *NY Daily News*

NEW YORK FUN FACT

Hottest Subway Station: Of the 12 hottest stations surveyed by the New York Daily News, the 95th St. Bay Ridge Station of the R Line, turned out to have registered a brutal 100 degrees in August. Whew!

THE URBAN
GUERRILLA

Don't be shy if you do have a gripe to share with the TA. Did you know that the customer service department of the New York City Transit Authority receives more than 5,000 complaints every month at its Brooklyn headquarters? Next time try sending your complaint directly to: Jack Lusk, Senior Vice President for Customer Services -- NYCTA, 370 Jay Street, Brooklyn, NY 11201.

> There's a saying that the Independent subway line got it's name because it arrives whenever it wants to.

History of New York Subway Fare Increases

Year	Fare	Year	Fare
1904	$0.05	1981	$0.75
1953	$0.10	1984	$0.90
1966	$0.20	1986	$1.00
1970	$0.30	1990	$1.15
1972	$0.35	1992	$1.25
1975	$0.50	1995	$1.50
1980	$0.60	1997-8	????

BELLIGERENT BEGGARS
THE 6 BEST SPARE CHANGE LINES

The Best Panhandler in NYC at Making You Feel Guilty if You Pass Him By:

His name is Ezra. He resides on the Upper West Side of the city. Sometimes he can be seen on a bench relaxing and having a smoke, listening to his Walkman, or eating a slice of pizza. He's calm, relaxed, and to the naked eye just like you and I. However, when he's ready for his day's work of begging on the streets, and I do mean *begging*, no one I've seen panhandling in New York can match his performance.

Dressed in dirty T-shirt and trousers, his soliciting begins by lying down on the sidewalk, usually on upper Broadway. He whips himself into a round of intense sobbing (no tears), whining, and gut wrenching hysterics.

When someone stops to talk to him, he stops the dramatics and answers in a calm, friendly manner. He's open to an occasional conversation. But once they depart he slips back into character once again and is quite adept at making some New Yorkers part with their spare change.

These days having panhandlers in New York hit you up for spare change on a daily basis is just part and parcel of life in the big city. Invariably, the exchange is difficult at best. You feel guilty if you don't give or feel you've sold out if you do. Hearing the words, *"God bless"* or *"Have a nice day"* seems to take on another dimension. If this sentiment doesn't leave you with a tinge of guilt, just consider it a diplomatic "Screw you."

If you must give and are not sure where your money is going, groups for the homeless recommend a fast food gift certificate in place of cash. That way you can be moderately certain the money won't be used for drugs or alcohol, but just on plain old junk food.

The US Supreme Court upheld a ban against panhandling along with other solicitations in the subway. Those who do it repeatedly are subject to arrest. Straphangers proved to be a too captive and responsive audience, according to a recent survey.

The US Supreme Court has also ruled against panhandling in the Port Authority Bus Terminal (West 42nd St. & 8th Avenue), airports and the World Trade Center. But according to a recent US Court of Appeals ruling under the protection of the First Amendment, beggars can continue to ask for handouts on the streets of New York as long as it is done in a non-threatening manner.

AGGRESSIVE PANHANDLING

The City Council has recently passed Intro. 456-B, in September of 1996, which criminalizes aggressive panhandling in public places, as well as solicitations of motorists. This bill now give the police the authority to arrest squeegee people, aggressive panhandlers and beggars at automatic teller machines. Aggressive panhandling is defined as begging in a threatening manner involving physical contact or intentionally blocking pedestrian or vehicular traffic. Harassing behavior is defined as following a person about in a public place.

This bill now gives the police the power to make arrests without having to show that the beggars intended to be menacing, only that they were, the Mayor's criminal justice coordinator, Katie Lapp said in a recent interview. Formerly, the police had to prove intent. If convicted, the guilty party can get up to 16 days in jail and/or a fine up to $100. No brain surgeon needed here, but my guess is that if they had $100 to begin with, they wouldn't be panhandling.

GET A GRIP

- On the whole, New Yorkers have had it. Giving money on the street is now being referred to as "Chump Change." The recession and fear have made a good many people keep on walking or treat panhandlers with hostility. There are those who believe that avoiding eye contact works best, while others are convinced that merely acknowledging their solicitors is sufficient.

- Each panhandler has developed their own style. The good ones play on your emotions and feelings by whining, following and shouting. Seems though the more one gives, the more this outgrowth of urban decay lives on.

- Perhaps a smoother way of dealing with a request is to acknowledge it in some manner, instead of pretending the individual is not there, *i.e. "Sorry, not today."* New Yorkers are quite generous and don't mind occasional requests for handouts. But generosity suddenly turns to annoyance when faced with daily requests.

NOT EVEN WITH A 10 FOOT POLE --
NO BEGGING IN FRONT OF ATMS

The homeless have made the waiting areas of ATMs their headquarters. Up until recently these areas were unprotected and invited crime. However with the new law, no begging is allowed within 10 feet of a NYC ATM.

As expected, the ACLU and Coalition for the Homeless believe this legislation is unfair and continue to oppose it.

Kansas City has one of the toughest anti-panhandling laws in the nation. There the practice is outlawed completely. Other cities like San Francisco, Seattle, Berkley and Atlanta are toughening up on street solicitations. Overall, people seem to be saying that they want their city back. In the meantime, it would be worthwhile to call your bank and voice your concern about their ATM area and the need for private security. If you're given the runaround, consider taking your business elsewhere and tell them so.

NEW YORK FUN FACT

Hold-ups at bank cash machines in the city have dropped from 380 in 1991 to 304 in 1993. In 1995 there were 193 robberies at ATMs in New York City. The drop is attributed to new camera surveillance, improved lighting, security guards, and locks because of new city requirements .

TOP 6 NEW YORK SPARE CHANGE LINES
(all overheard and all for real)

① *I'm on the road to hell. Would you help me pay the toll?*

② *I'm Johnny Cash's brother -- No cash!*

③ *Any spare change? My building is going co-op.*

④ *I'm a hospital nurse and I need two dollars for baby formula.*

⑤ *Would you like to contribute to the United Negro Pizza Fund?*

⑥ *Pleeeeeeeeeeeeeeeeeeeeeeeeeeeeeeeeeeease!!!*

ONLY IN THE NAKED CITY

As a variation on panhandling, I once saw two young women with pierced noses standing on the corner of West 8th and Broadway doing what only happens in New York.

They stood with a cardboard cup full of coins asking passerbys if *they* wanted any spare change. I stood and watched for half an hour. Not one New Yorker stopped to accept a nickel.

KEY CHARITIES

Community Service Society of NY
105 East 22nd Street
New York, NY 10010

Federation of Protestant Welfare Agencies
281 Park Avenue South
New York, NY 10010

UJA-Federation of New York
130 East 59th Street, Rm. 427
Mew York, NY 10022

Contributions are tax deductible on Federal, State & City income taxes.

NEW YORK FUN FACT

There were a staggering 996 arrests for panhandling in the subway during the banner year 1994.

However only 81 arrests were made July 1995 to June 1996.

Are things getting better or are the cops getting lazier?

#27

ATTACK OF THE
SQUEEGEE PEOPLE

You've just been greeted at the stoplight with a wet, soapy something-or-other on your car. An outstretched arm proceeds to lather up the windshield while you're busy flailing your arms in a frenzy. Suddenly you discover that you can't see a thing and are asked for a donation -- or else. Getting "squeegeed" has become common practice at city intersections these days whether you like it or not.

Generally this ritual is performed by a street person who approaches your car while you're waiting for the traffic light to change. That's the sign post up ahead -- you've just entered "The Squeegee Zone."

Some squeegee folk tend to be more aggressive than others. Some ask first if they can wash your windshield, while others just plunge right in. While some motorists believe that the best defense is to turn on their windshield wipers in an effort to discourage the squeegist, the Crime Prevention Bureau of the Police Department doesn't think this a terribly good idea.

GET A GRIP

- Some squeegee enthusiasts, after being held at bay by a set of windshield wipers in motion, have been known to bend them in an effort of one-upmanship. It's happened more than once.

- Your best route on this one is to wave him off. If he doesn't listen and hits your windshield with something wet *don't* get out of your car. Confronting him is one of the worst things you can do. Your particular squeegist might be on crack, just plain cracked, or very possibly *more* disgruntled than you are with life in New York. You might also leave yourself wide open for a belt in the mouth or worse yet, a carjacking.

- You have no obligation to tip the squeegist for their efforts. That of course is a matter of discretion. However in some cases, I've personally witnessed some windshields getting hit with a big soapy sponge and *no* squeegee to follow. More often, if you can bear being called an obscenity or two, (for New Yorkers that's just an average day) drive on.

In September of 1996, the City Council recently passed Local Law # 80 which criminalizes aggressive panhandling in public places, as well as solicitations of motorists. This bill now give the police the authority to arrest squeegee people, aggressive panhandlers and beggars at automatic teller machines.

NEW YORK FUN FACT

THE SQUEEGEE ZONES

- Bowery & FDR Drive
- Bowery & Houston Street
- 41st Street & 9th Avenue (coming out of Lincoln Tunnel)
- 42nd Street & 9th Avenue (coming out of Lincoln Tunnel)
- 48th Street & West Side Highway
- 56th Street & West Side Highway
- Watts Street & Avenue of Americas (going west into Holland Tunnel)
- First & Willis Avenues
- FDR Drive & 96th Street
- York Avenue & 62nd Street

THE URBAN GUERRILLA

If you're bothered by this nuisance repeatedly, try buying an FBI light, aka "teardrop light" available at most hardware or lighting stores (check out the ones on Canal Street) in different colors.

Keep it handy when you drive. In the event of any oncoming squeegee attack, just whip out your flashing light and put it on the dashboard. It's guaranteed to ward off any persistence pests. Throw in a bull horn and you got it made.

RECENT DEVELOPMENTS

As of late, the Police Department has been aggressively cracking down on this illegal practice. Numerous arrests have followed and enforcement remains aggressive. The rationale is that those who commit these small crimes move on to perpetrate larger ones.

Whether the same vigorous enforcement will continue and whether we have seen an end to the squeegee people remains to be seen.

PART FOUR

INFORMATION

IS

POWER

#28   WHERE TO GET A LAWYER QUICKLY AND FOR FREE

For those New Yorkers in need of free legal advice, the New York Bar Association Referral Line, *626-7373*, will help answer your legal questions. For whatever they can't answer, they refer private attorneys whose specialties are in different areas (half hour consultations are $25). The referral line operates Monday through Friday from 9 am - 5:30 p.m., *closed on holidays.*

The Bar Association *also* provides the *Monday Night Law Clinic,* from 5:30 p.m. to 7:30 p.m., located at the Bar Association, 36 West 44th Street., between Fifth and Avenue of the Americas, room 310. It is a free consultation with a lawyer on such legal matters as bankruptcy, consumer credit, landlord-tenant, family, and labor problems.

You *must* call first and make an appointment if you wish to attend the Monday Night Law Clinic. Consultations last about 30 minutes and you should come prepared with contracts, papers, and any other relevant information so that your consultation time is put to good use.

KEY NUMBERS

- *New York Bar Assoc.* (9 am-5:30 p.m.)   626-7373
Legal Clinic and Referral

- *NYS Dept. Disciplinary Committee*   685-1000
- *Character & Fitness Committee,*
Appellate Div. Supreme Court   779-1779
(To check to see if your lawyer is in good standing)

#29

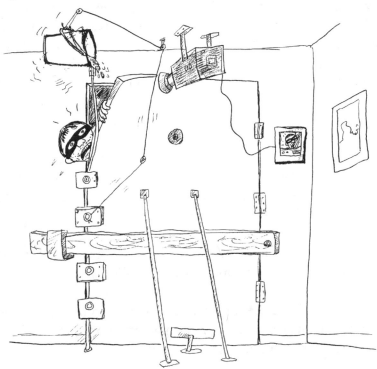

WHAT TO LOOK OUT FOR
BEFORE GOING TO A LOCKSMITH

Just because you purchased the best lock in town doesn't necessarily mean you'll be protected. Today, more and more thieves learn to overcome obstacles just as fast as they're developed. What's surprising is how many folks fail to change the lock the landlord furnishes them with. Just how many keys for these locks are floating around is anybody's guess.

In a recent year, 90,000 residents reported burglaries in New York City. Amazingly, this figure represents a sharp decline from preceding years. However, it does not reflect the large amount of burglaries that go unreported every year.

Based on interviews with security personnel and locksmiths in the metropolitan area the following preventative measures are highly recommended:

☞ First, before equipping your refuge with a security arsenal -- you want to find the right locksmith. Check with other neighbors in your building or at work and go by personal recommendations.

☞ Next, make sure your locksmith is licensed by the Department of Consumer Affairs, (487-4379).

☞ Check with the Better Business Bureau to see if they've been given a satisfactory or unsatisfactory rating (533-6200). Stop trouble before it starts.

☞ Check their references. It is advisable not just to drop in on any ol' locksmith who happens to be in the area. Locksmiths, like other trade folk, are not always licensed, and if you do have a problem afterwards you could find yourself up a creek.

☞ "Consider the door to your apartment and more importantly the frame of the door itself. If your door frame was once broken and not repaired properly, you leave yourself wide open for a potential problem no matter what lock you buy," says locksmith Willie Flores of the American Security Association. Flores emphasizes the need to inspect the frame of the door on the *inside* of the apartment.

What you're checking for is to see that it's solid, in place, and not patched up in any section. If you discover that it is, you are advised to talk to your landlord (another pleasant chore) and get him to replace it in it's entirety. Wooden frames are the most vulnerable.

☛ Once your door frame is sturdy, your next step is to determine the condition of the door to your home. If it's in crummy shape, once again it doesn't matter how much money you spend on your new lock. Your security is compromised.

☛ It is highly advisable to have a Kalamein door (a fireproof metal covered wood door), a hollow metal door, or a solid wood door at the very least. Some apartments in the city still have closet doors which provide the *least* protection of all. Have these replaced as soon as possible.

☛ Closet doors can be punched or kicked in by just about anybody in moderately good health. Get your landlord to give you a solid door or split the cost with him so he doesn't have a heart attack.

LOCK INSTALLATION

☛ Always have two locks at least 18" apart from one another on your door.

☛ The Deadbolt surface lock or tubular Deadbolt with a pick-proof Medeco cylinder; a minimum of six pins is recommended. The more pins, the more pick resistant. Having two locks on your door is better than one.

☞ The Medeco Bodyguard with Steel Guard or the D-11 drop-bolt lock are also good choices. Incidentally, everything can be gotten into sooner or later -- even bank vaults! If somebody wants to get into your home badly enough they will find a way. All you can do is slow them down. For most criminals, choosing the path of least resistance suits their purpose.

☞ By taking these safeguards, you'll discourage the burglar's efforts and make their ventures a hell of a lot more time-consuming. Time is usually the name of the game.

GET A GRIP

• A theft-deterring key card is a good idea to have these days. It must be presented to the locksmith with identification before a key can be duplicated. Also invest in a good window lock that will secure to the sill. For the doorknob consider a mortise lock

• When investing in a window gate, it is advisable that you purchase a "Ferry" or "Safety Gate" which is approved by the Board of Standards. Avoid "Scissor" or "Accordion" gates which require a padlock. In an emergency situation the pins inside the lock melt and trap you inside.

• Get a peephole that has an 180 degree view and that cannot be unscrewed from the outside.

- Put a secure metal weather strip on the bottom of your apartment door. By taking as many precautions as possible, you're slowing down the threat of a burglary when *"time is money."*

- *Never* invest in a double-sided lock for any part of your home. Besides it being illegal, this lock is **not** intended for your residence. It requires a key to unlock. Some folks have locked themselves in under the worst of circumstances. The heat from a nearby fire has been known to melt the pins inside the lock, trapping you like a rat. These locks are occasionally used for commercial establishments where there is little or no traffic, never is it recommended for a residence!

KEY NUMBERS

- *Department of Consumer Affairs*   487-4398

- *Better Business Bureau*   533-6200

(LOCKSMITHS OPEN 24 HOURS)

- Village Locksmiths
615 Hudson St.   362-7000
- Associated Locksmith
1138 Lexington   628-9700
- A & Z Locksmith
Fifth Av. & 46th   535-8900
- Manhattan All Star Locksmiths
300 E 34th St.   406-1260

#30

RELENTLESS ROACHES

As a boy growing up in the East New York section of Brooklyn, I was no stranger to cockroaches. They were like the junkman, the soda truck, and the guy selling knishes by the schoolyard. They were fixtures of the neighborhood.

Roaches were in your bathroom, in your breakfast cereal, and sometimes in your bed. The most vivid memory I have on the subject was as a boy one summer morning. It was a very rainy day. My grandfather was about to take me to the corner where I would be boarding a bus for day camp.

Grandpa always kept his umbrella in a corner of the hallway where it was dark and dank. He never really had reason to use his umbrella since he was retired and didn't wander too far from home. Most of his days now were spent in front of the television set watching programs like "My Little Margie", and "Topper".

Unbeknownst to him, after many months, the roaches had found refuge in his old umbrella.

The rain poured down mercilessly. He walked me, his ten-year-old grandson, to the front stoop of his brownstone, where he proceeded to open his umbrella above us and I witnessed something I'll never forget.

What seemed like billions of roaches came cascading out of the umbrella onto the wet pavement. In droves, without end, they continued to drop like the rain itself. Crawling across the metal skeleton of the umbrella and down the shaft. Dropping from the skies on that rain-soaked day in 1959. They scurried for shelter, not knowing what had become of their sanctuary. Roaches to the left of me, roaches to the right of me, underfoot and running in a panic searching frantically for another umbrella to hide in.

When I first moved into my studio apartment on West 72nd Street some sixteen years later, I never forgot that image. The building I moved into was pre-war, rent stabilized, and complete with roaches. I went to extremes to make it off limits to our little friends. Sealing up every last little crack and crevice with plaster, I painstakingly sprayed, painted, and stuffed steel wool into any hole. I especially made sure not to keep my umbrella in the corner of the room.

Months went by and I never once saw a roach anywhere within my new apartment. After listening patiently to horror stories from others, I was now feeling a tinge of guilt. It was as if word had gotten out in the roach community that my place was beneath contempt. It got so I had this recurring nightmare. I'd come home tired one night from work. I'd walk into the kitchen for a beer, flick on the light and find a 550 pound roach in battle fatigues waiting for me.

I guess the point of all this is, you can never kill all the roaches in the world but you *can* make your apartment roach-free.

For some New Yorkers, the only wildlife they'll ever encounter are the roaches which invade their homes. You spray and sweep, even go ballistic with roach hotels and condominiums only to discover our little friends coming back for more. Roaches are one of the few species around that run neck and neck with New Yorkers when it comes to being experts on survival in the big city.

Cockroaches happen to be one of the oldest living insects in the world. They haven't changed a bit after a mere 350 million years. There are close to 60 different kinds of cockroaches in the United States and New York may have some of the toughest. In fact, I've been told there's a cockroach museum somewhere in the midwest -- even though we New Yorkers instinctively know it belongs right here.

Let's begin with a few facts: roaches carry filth on their legs and spread disease by walking over food or leaving their bowel movements in food. They also leave behind a dark colored fluid that they vomit from their mouths when eating. Unless dishes are thoroughly washed before using, their bowel movements mixed with this dark colored material will give off a foul odor once warm food is put in the dish.

If you haven't guessed it by now, cockroaches are a health menace and can spread Salmonella, an infection causing severe stomach cramps, diarrhea, nausea and vomiting. They have been found to carry many diseases including fungal and viral disease, tuberculosis, dysentery and many other types of germs. Of the almost 60 types of cockroaches, just four in New York cause the most difficulty.

A NEW YORK CITY CAST OF CHARACTERS

- *The Oriental Cockroach* is black or very dark brown, often called a *"waterbug"* because it prefers damp places. This so-called *"waterbug"* is really a cockroach, no matter how diligently he argues otherwise.

- *The American Cockroach* is a reddish-brown color and is found in sewers or on first floors of buildings. This little devil can fly and can grow from 1 1/2 to 2 inches long.

- *The Brown Bandit Cockroach* is about 1/2 inch long and has two bands of brownish-yellow color on the wing. This guy can be found all over the house, in cupboards, pantries, furniture, bedrooms and bathrooms. Warning: it will *fly* into your home.

- *The German Cockroach* is light brown in color and about 5/8 inches long. He can be found all over the house but is usually found in kitchens and bathrooms. (*Not a fussy eater.*)

SOME STOMACH-TURNING FACTS

☛ Cockroaches like to live in dirt and filth. When food, temperature, and moisture conditions are just right, they multiply rapidly. However, if good housekeeping and sanitation are practiced, roaches usually find some other place to live (*perhaps at your noisy neighbor's condo*), or they just bite the dust.

☛ Besides identifying the adult, it is also important for you to spot the eggs. These are laid in a leathery pouch which the female forms at the end of her body. The female drops its egg pouch before it's ready to hatch. About 30 roaches hatch from these pouches. The egg pouches can be compared in aspect to a small dark pinto bean.

☛ The Brown Bandit roach will hide its pouches by sticking them under cabinets, surfaces, and drawers. If you see this in your home, it would be wise of you to hunt for their eggs -- even though it may not be Easter!

GET A GRIP

☛ Roaches can enter your house by way of boxes and bags that you bring home from shopping. I recommend that you fold all paper bags flat, then "iron" them with the side of your fist. I know it sounds silly, but it works. Roaches hide in bags and cartons. Check any you bring into your house.

☛ You can also put the bag under your feet and do the "New York Stomp" on it to make sure nothing crawls out. Try to do this procedure when you're alone. If anybody asks what you're doing, tell them you have a sudden urge to do the tango. It really does help.

☛ Seal up all cracks in your home on floors and walls, baseboards, or where pipes comes into your home. You can use plaster, putty, or Plastic Wood for this.

☛ Use sprays and powders in limited applications. Don't treat *entire* walls, floors and ceilings with them. Treat only along the baseboard, under the cupboards and similar places where they hide. Don't treat areas where food is prepared or stored. Be very careful around pet areas. Sprays cannot take the place of good clean housekeeping.

☛ Many restaurants, stores, and homes have occasional roaches every so often. Despite all the precautions taken, you shouldn't self-flagellate and feel guilty if you experience one of their visits. There's no reason, however, to allow an infestation to develop. Kill the little creeps at once.

THE URBAN
GUERRILLA

On the end of their bodies, roaches have two tiny points called "cerci." It is extremely difficult to sneak up on a cockroach because the cerci feel even the slightest movements of air. An entomologist who makes studying cockroaches her life's work had this piece of advice: "When lights are out for a while, flick on the kitchen or bathroom light to see where the little bugger goes back to. Then go after its home which is sure to have more inhabitants. Take a flashlight and examine all cracks and crevices to find the key nesting area."

If you find that you can't control the situation, pest control companies licensed by the state may be the next step.

NEW YORK FUN FACTS

Cockroaches can last a month without water and for three months without food. They live *everywhere* except the polar regions. For every roach you see, there are at least 12 that you don't see hiding in the walls.

E. Randy Dupree of the Health Deptartment's Bureau of Pest control said in a recent interview that there are 8 million rats living in the 5 boroughs. That comes to 1 rat per person. Have you met *your* rat today?

Remember -- your landlord must have your apartment fumigated if you request it. This is covered under the Warranty of Habitibility Code.

KEY NUMBERS

- *Housing Preservation & Development*   960-4800
  (for residential roach complaints)
- *Central Complaint Bureau (Dept. of Health)* 442-1838
  (complaints about rats and gabage)
- *Pest Control (Dept. of Health)*   718-956-7103
  (residential inspections)
- *Commercial Inspections*   334-7761
- *State Environmental Conservation*   718-482-4994
  (to see if exterminator is state licensed)

#31

"Reality is the leading cause of stress..."
Jane Wagner
The Search for Intelligent Life in the Universe

I LOVE THE SMELL OF STRESS
IN THE MORNING

If you live or work in this city and are between the ages of 30 and 65, chances are you're getting enough...of *stress* that is. If not for stress who would be our daily companion in New York? Maybe its the guy in the knit hat who's been following us for the last nine blocks.

Most of us know what it's like to be against the wall on a day to day basis. We're always allowing others to press our buttons.

Stress happens when we try to do too many things at once. That includes career, finances, and anything vaguely passing as a social life. When we bite off too much to chew and think we can handle it, that's where the trouble starts.

Here are some early symptoms of the existence of stress (in New York and elsewhere):

- *Irritability*
- *Lack of concentration*
- *Difficulty sleeping*

You increase your susceptibility to infection when you're under the gun. Often it results in neckaches, backaches, chest pains, palpitations, peptic ulcers, diabetes, cancer, rheumatoid arthritis, and bowel spasms. If you're not paying attention to what your body is telling you, you increase your vulnerability to a disease or ailment when your body knuckles under. Heart attack, stroke, depression and other surprises may be just around the corner.

SOME SIGNS THAT YOU'RE NOT HANDLING STRESS WELL

☒ Pathological fatigue
☒ Gastro-intestinal complaints
☒ Insomnia
☒ Trouble maintaining relationships
☒ Upper respiratory infections
☒ Rising blood pressure
☒ Inability to concentrate
☒ Loss of libido

Not having any way of countering these signs can contribute to early deterioration and premature aging. If you're skipping meals, eat in a hurry, dine on things you shouldn't and overindulge with alcohol -- you're on your way to an early grave.

GET A GRIP

- Treatment for stress begins with nutrition. Stabilize your eating pattern. Don't skip meals, especially breakfast, because that's where you get 1/4 of your daily calories. Incidentally, coach, breakfast doesn't mean a prune danish and a Diet Pepsi.

- Get in the habit of exercising. It makes you feel better and relieves the tension. Get involved with a stress workshop which will help you understand what makes you blow your top.

- Overall, nutrition is the key to managing stress. None of us can totally avoid stress but we can help lessen what is depleted in our bodies when stress hits us. Nutrition will help one be more resilient and more resistant to it. The best way to blow it health-wise is to ignore your body's warnings and what you're shoveling into it.

TOP 10 WORST FAST FOODS
(based on fat and sodium content)

10. Quaker 100% Natural Cereal   5. Oscar Mayer Lunchables
9. Gwaltney Chicken Franks   4. Haagen Daaz ice cream
8. A Plain Cake Dunkin Donut   3. Campbell's regular soups
7. Nissin Noodles with Shrimp   2. Rice-a-Roni chicken w/ve
6. Movie Theater Popcorn   1. Contadina Alfredo sauce

Source: Center for Science in the Public Interest

Dishonorable mention: Entenmann's donuts, Kung Pao
Chicken, Granola Cereal, Taco Bell's Taco Salad.

The Center for Science in the Public Interest warns that
eating foods that are high in fat as well as those that have
high sodium contents can result in heart disease,
hypertension, diabetes, and obesity.

*Provide yourself with the best possible resources to cope
with whatever New York City throws your way.*

NEW YORK STRESS BUSTERS
How To Get a Handle On It

- Practice either yoga, meditation, bio-feedback, or
  positive imagery.

- Exercise regularly. It breaks up tension in the muscles
  and releases relaxing chemicals in your brain.

- Get adequate sleep and rest.

- Don't work through lunch if you can help it.

- Avoid self-medication like alcohol and sedatives.

- Cultivate friendships. Have someone to talk things over with.

- Laughter is essential. Visit a comic.

- Take small breaks during the day.

- Keep your resume updated and be prepared.

According to recent medical research, if you have one or more of the following, your chance of premature death or disability, up to 70 years of age drops down to 1/3.

☞ Marriage or primary relationship
☞ Friends
☞ Spiritual Relief

Note: 1/3 don't survive their first heart attack.

KEY NUMBERS

- *Lenox Hill Relaxation Tape*
24 hr access: 434-3200
                                                                        ext. 272

- *Lenox Hill Hospital Relaxation Booth*
open Mon-Fri, 9:30 am -- 4:30 PM
Corner 76th & Lexington Avenue   434-2980
(free)

- *Stress Reduction Workshops*   434-3150
  Lenox Hill Hospital
  100 East 77th Street
($15 for two hour session. Phone for schedule)
* The hospital also offers free nutritional counseling
by a registered dietitian every Tuesday at 2 p.m.   434-2981

- *Columbia Presbyterian/Eastside Lecture Series*
Free Lectures on a wide variety of medical topics.
The featured speakers are members of the faculty.
Reserve a seat, seating is limited.   439-1323

- *The Great American BackRub Store*
  Locations throughout the city   800-BACKRUB
(About $10 for 10 minutes, they even have a
Deluxe Scalp Treatment for an additional $3.95)

- *The Sleep Line*   434-3200
guidelines for natural (drug-free) sleep   ext. SLP

- *9 to 5 Job Survival Hotline*   800-522-0925
counseling, advice

THE URBAN
GUERRILLA

After a hard and stressful day, why not treat yourself to a massage? Your muscles will have a chance to be cleansed of toxins. Inflammation will be relieved, and besides it just feels good.

A good massage cleanses the tissues, improves circulation and relieves tension. Be good to yourself.

RECENT DEVELOPMENTS

Call 1-800-94-MASSAGE to have a massage within the privacy of your home. *The Quiet Touch* is made up of a network of licensed massage therapists who promise to deliver a massage anywhere in the United States within one hour. They charge $85 per hour, but ask them to send you a coupon which brings the price down to $60. Corporate rates are also available.

#32

PET STRESS IN THE CITY

A one to one relationship with a pet provides many benefits to the beleaguered New Yorker. Just petting your dog or cat helps lower your blood pressure, reduces stress, and may very well save your life. Having a pet nearby can be of great consolation. But what it may surprise you to learn is that in this city, your pet may be walking the same urban tightrope as you.

"Cats in Manhattan are more on the edge. More so than in other places because many New Yorkers live in the fast lane. Cats (as well as other animals) are very much affected by the people they live with," states cat therapist Carole Wilbourn, herself a New Yorker.

A good deal of the stress an animal may experience in the city might have to do with the frenetic lifestyle of the owner. Depending on the personality of your animal, it might respond with its own deviant behavior.

Ms. Wilbourn, who teaches a course on "Understanding Your Cat" in the city says, "You might say it's the ripple effect because cats as well as dogs are affected by body language and tone of voice. If a person comes home and they're feeling tense and distraught, an animal picks up on it. Especially an indoor cat, because it can't go out and take a walk somewhere. It's environment is static and more so if it's thin-skinned," she said. Some city conditions may add to the problem.

A pet behaviorist for the Animal Medical Center, Dr. Peter Borchelt believes that 99% of these problems are solvable. "It would be a disaster to have people put their dogs and cats to sleep for treatable problems," says Borchelt. He does make clear that approximately one third of the cases he is called in on involve dogs that suffer from a separation anxiety disorder. "You have to gradually get them used to your not being there is small doses," he said.

Pet Expert Warren Eckstein believes your pet can also suffer from noise phobia. Sounds such as loud sirens, trucks backfiring, fireworks, etc. cause your pet to become nervous and try to escape to anyplace in your apartment where they can seek refuge. "Dogs may try to soothe themselves by chewing on items around the house or even on themselves. Cats may scratch the sofa or the wallpaper. If your pet's extremely nervous he may vomit or suffer from diarrhea."

RESOLVING NOISE PHOBIAS

Mr. Eckstein believes that you should gradually condition your pet for loud noises, so he won't be shell shocked the next time.   As an example "Turn your radio on at a reasonably high volume during any noise so that it will help drown out the sound."

The process is very gradual and if your pet lives in dread of specific sounds, such as thunderstorms, firecrackers, etc., "getting a sound effects tape and playing it a little bit each day gradually increasing the volume in an effort to desensitize him to it" recommends Mr. Eckstein. "Don't rush him into it and make matters worse. The emphasis is on being gradual. Hopefully soon he will be paying absolutely no attention to the sound."

Mr. Eckstein also believes in the importance of soothing and reassuring your pet when he's frightened, or diverting his attention by playing his favorite game.

So what can you do to reduce your best friend's stress factor in the world's largest pressure cooker? The best way to deal with the problem is before it even starts. Your animal offers you unconditional love and is always there for you. So here are some guidelines to follow before 'Peaches' or 'Jungle Baby' gets up on the couch and into pet therapy.

6 DE-STRESSING GUIDELINES
FOR YOUR PET AND YOU

1. When you leave your home each day, make sure to see your pet's face. You don't want to have a small cat or dog locked in the closet. When you leave in the morning and you have said a good word or good-bye to your pet, you'll be off to a good start.

2. Ms. Wilbourn suggests leaving a message for your cat or dog on your answering machine. The sound of your voice will give your cat a very good feeling. Your co-workers may think you're *loony tunes* but evidently it can make a difference.

3. Have either a neighbor or sitter visit or walk your pooch if you know you're going to be late on certain nights.

4. If you're having someone new move in, whether it's a roommate, lover, or crazy uncle Harry, spend some time with your animals with that new person so that your pets feel included.

5. When you get home at night, give your pet a big hug.

   Warning: This is __not__ advisable for goldfish, falcons, or boa constrictors. In those cases a simple, "How's it going"? will suffice.

6. Be sure to do something good for yourself, i.e., go to the zoo, put on relaxing music, take a bubble bath, get a massage. Your pet will actually benefit from your behavior.

YOUR TENANT PET RIGHTS

These days most standard residential leases, including rent stabilized and cooperative proprietary leases, have a no-pet clause. The 'pet waiver' law contained in the New York City Administrative Code deals with tenant pet possession rights.

The law states that when a tenant has a pet in violation of their lease, the landlord has a period of 3 months within which to serve the tenant with court papers seeking the removal of the pet. These papers are called the Notice of Petition.

If the landlord does not take any action during this 3-month period, the tenant can keep the pet for the duration of the lease and all renewal periods. The 3-month period begins when the landlord finds out about the pet.

NUISANCE PROCEEDING

If your dog barks continuously, is off the leash and waters various parts of the hallways or lobby, your landlord can take action against you under a nuisance proceeding. This is defined as an ongoing pattern of conduct that interferes with the use and enjoyment of another tenant's home.

This action is separate and apart from the NYC Administrative Code. If your case goes to court, the judge will give you a period of time to correct the problem. If on the other hand you fail to do so, your landlord can evict you.

Try to see the problem from your neighbor's point of view. Keep the lines of communication open. The courts have recognized how valuable the warmth love of a pet is to many New York City tenants, especially the elderly and disabled.

For more information contact:
Ms. Maddy Tarnofsky c/o Friends of Animals   932-9787
(attorney, specializing in protecting tenants with pets)

KEY NUMBERS

• *Animal Medical Center*   838-8100
24 hr emergency treatment, 365 days
62nd Street & York Ave

• *Dr. Peter Borchelt,*
  Animal Behaviorist   718-891-4200

• *Park East Animal Hospital*   832-8417
  24 hr emergencies 52 East 64th St.

• *Animal Poison Control*   340-4494

• *Nat'l Animal Poison Control Ctr.*   800-548-2423

• *Cat Therapist, Carole Wilbourn*   741-0397

• *ASPCA*   876-7700
92nd Street & York Avenue

• *Pet Taxi*
  227 East 56th St.   755-1757

• *Pet Ambulance*   491-5300

- *Humane Society*   752-4840
306 E. 59th Street

- *Bide A Wee*   532-4455
410 E. 38th Street   532-5884

Pet Health Insurance

- *Veterinary Pet Insurance (VPI)*   800-USA-PETS

#33

HOW NOT TO GET NAILED
AT THE SALON

Never has "doing your nails" been quite as popular and affordable as it is today in one of the many nail salons in the city. More recently, an influx of Korean-owned nail salons (at last count 1300 citywide) have been burgeoning in every conceivable neighborhood. They employ large groups of women whose soul function is to turn out a manicure in 10-15 minutes flat, cuticles included.

The newer salons, springing up all over the city, give pause to the older European nail salons which traditionally take more time with their customers but are known to charge much higher rates.

BEWARE!

According to some of the manicurists interviewed in the city, it takes too long to sterilize instruments by using either Barbicide (a brand of sterilization solution) or heat sterilization, when turnover is the name of the game.

GET A GRIP

- One of the things you should check to see is just how clean the establishment appears to be. Second, see if they sterilize their instruments *before* each new customer and not just at the end of the day.

- Make sure the nail salon you're going to uses clean water, fresh cotton swabs, and new emery boards. Don't be afraid to question. Remember, acrylic nails are not advisable. These nails do not let your own nails breathe under the acrylic. Add a little water under the acrylic nail and the result is infection.

Up until July 5, 1994, no nail salon in New York State was required to be licensed. No minimum requirement in training is needed to open a business. If you do have a complaint, the Department of State has become the new licenser for nail salons, beauty and barber shops, real estate brokers, hearing aid dealers, fire alarm installers and security guards.

NEW YORK FUN FACT

In many instances, Korean-based nail salons charge higher rates for men's manicures. Manicurists say that a man's nails require more work and time.

Then again women have traditionally paid more for their dry cleaning and haircuts. So perhaps this evens the score.

Consumer rights activists: get your local leaders to sponsor gender-based anti-discrimination legislation on these matters. Councilmember Karen Koslowitz (D) of Queens heads the Consumer Rights Committee. 718-544-3212

 KEY NUMBERS

- *Dept. Of State (Licenser)*   417-5748

- *Dept. Of Health*   442-1999
  (Sanitary-related complaints)

- *Dept. Of Consumer Affairs*   498-4398
  (Overcharging)

Get a Grip: For those rude merchants -- In Korean the words, 'MANO-GA-UP-SA-NEE-DA' means, 'you have *no* manners'.

HOSPITAL EMERGENCY ROOMS ALWAYS OPEN
(and shortest waiting times)

As someone whose waited in emergency rooms for hours on end, I can tell you that it's no picnic. You begin your wait by leafing through hospital magazines -- some that date back to the McKinley Administration. You get up from your seat, go to the receptionist and remind her that you've been waiting since the high holy days. She in turn tells you that there are several people ahead of you. The guy with the mothball stuck in his ear, the woman with the tire marks on her scalp and the attending physician who was sucked into the air shaft.

When I researched the information for this chapter, I spoke with not only heads of emergency rooms but nurses and attending staff in the line of duty.

Listed below are the names, addresses, phone numbers, and least crowded times of 7 of New York City's 24-hour NYC emergency rooms.

Bear in mind that the "least crowded time to go" information should not be used to postpone an emergency.

Middle of the night aside, some emergency rooms have listed daytime alternate hours.

- **Cabrini Medical Centre**   227 E 19th St (2-3 Aves)
  995-6620
  (*least crowded hours: 3 am - 5 am*)

- **Mount Sinai Hospital**   W 100th St & Madison Av
  241-7171
  (*least crowded hours: 2 am -5 am or 7 am -9 pm*)

- **Roosevelt Hospital**   59th St (9-10th Aves)
  523-6800
  (*least crowded hours: 7 am - 9 am*)

- **St. Luke's Hospital Centre**   W113th St & Amsterdam
  523-3343
  (*least crowded hours: 4 am - 8 am*)

- **St. Vincent's Hospital**   W 11th St & 7th Ave
  604-7997
  (*least crowded times: 2 am - 4 am or 6 am - 7 am*)

- NY Hospital Cornell Med Ctr   York Ave & East River
    746-5050
    (least crowded times: 6 am - 7:30 am)

- Urgent Care Ctr NY Hospital   York Ave & East River
    746-0795
    (For minor injuries) Mon-Fri 9 am - 9 pm
    In and out average time: 2 hours. Sunday closed

- NYU College of Dentistry   345 E 24th St (1st Ave)
    998-9856
    (least crowded hours: 8 am - 11 am or after 5:30 pm)
    998-9800

Other Hospitals

- Bellevue Hospital
    First Avenue and 27th Street   561-4141

- Beth Israel Health Care
    170 East End Avenue (87)   870-9000

- Coler Memorial Hospital
    Roosevelt Island   848-6000

- Columbia Presbyterian
    622 W. 168th St.   305-2500

- Goldwater Memorial
    Roosevelt Island   318-8000

- Harlem Hospital
    506 Lenox Ave.   939-1000

- Lenox Hill
  100 E. 77th St. - Park Avenue   434-2000

- Manhattan Psychiatric Center
  600 E. 125th St.   369-0500

- Metropolitan
  1901 First Ave.   423-6262

- Mount Sinai
  Fifth Avenue and 100th St.   241-6500

- New York Eye and Ear Infirmary
  Second Avenue and 14th St.   979-4472

- New York Downtown
  170 William Street   312-5000

- Hospital for Special Surgery
  535 E. 70th St.   606-1555

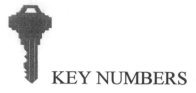

KEY NUMBERS

- *Dept. Of Health,*
  Div. of Professional Misconduct   613-2650
  (Complaints)

- *DOH Commissioner'S office*   788-5257

- *Access-a-Ride Transportation Program*   533-3700
  Disabled individuals or those who can't take public transportation. Call 718-694-3581 for application.
  (Access-A-Ride trips should be arranged 7 days in advance)

- *Health & Hospital Corporation*   788-9671
  Complaints regarding a Municipal Hospital

- *State Dept of Health's Hospital Unit*   613-4855
  Complaints regarding a Private Hospital

#35

WHERE TO PARK YOUR CAR
CHEAPLY AND OTHER SHOCKERS

No, I'm not sugguesting the bottom of the East River or atop a garbage dump in Staten Island. But you'd be shocked by the price discrepancies amongst private garages surveyed in Manhattan alone. Just one hour of parking in New York can run as much as $16.00 -- or if you know where to go, a mere $4.23. The leg work has been done -- now the choice is yours.

I've put together the least expensive garages and parking lots I've found in just about every part of Manhattan. Some are a little off the beaten path, others, right under your nose.

All rates are as of September 1996 as verified by personal visitation. All are indoor garages unless specified with (O) -- which specifies "parking lot."

BATTERY PARK

Construction Pl. Parking (O)	any 12 hrs	$12
142 West Street		
Betw. Murray-Vesey Sts.		
24 hrs.		

WALL STREET

Seaport Parking	all day	$10.15
Pearl Street & Peck Slip		

LITTLE ITALY

29 Mulberry Street		
24 hrs.	Any 12 hrs.	$ 7.61

SOHO

TJJ Auto Repair (O)	all day	$10.15
432 Broome St. Cor. Crosby		
8 am - 6 pm		

Quik Park (O)	1 hour	$ 5.29
37 West Houston	2 hours	8.88
Betw. Wooster & Greene	10 hours	11.84
8 am - Midnight		

WEST VILLAGE

Mutual	1 hour	$ 4.23
166 Perry Street	2 hours	5.92
Betw. Washington & West	up to 8 hrs	8.46
24 hrs. *Special Rates:*	*6 am - 6 pm*	*5.92*

Perry Garage	1 hour	$4.23
738 Greenwich Street	2 hours	6.77
Betw. Perry & West 11th	5-24 hours	13.52
24 hrs. *Special Rates:*	6 am - 6 pm	6.77

CHELSEA

First Parking (O)	1 hour	$6.55
23rd St - Ave of Americas	2 hours	7.82
7 am - 7 pm	12 hours	10.15
Sat	7 am - 5 pm	5.07

Stavros Parking (O)	1 hour	$5.26
748 Ave of Americas (24)	2 hours	6.14
24 hrs.	Max to 6 pm	8.46

MIDTOWN EAST

Horizon Garage	1 hour	$4.39
415 East 37th Street	3 hours	5.26
Betw. 1st & FDR Drive	10 hours	9.65
24 hrs. *Special Rates*	12 hours	9.25
Sat- Sun	12 hours	5.20

MIDTOWN WEST

38 West 33rd Corp.	any 10 hours	$9.94
between 5 & 6 Aves		
24 hrs.		

Turban Realities	1 hour	$4.44
401 West 42nd St	2 hours	6.34
Betw. 9th & 10th Aves	12 hours	8.03
24 hrs.	24 hours	9.73
Sun - Thurs	5 pm - 8 am	3.59

Quality Parking (O)	1 hour	$4.23
504 West 46th St (10th Ave)	10 hours	5.92
	12 hours	6.76

UPPER WEST SIDE

| West End Towers | any 12 hours | $5.07 |
| 62nd St & West End Ave | | |

*Lincoln Towers	1 hour	$4.02
205 West End Ave (70)	2 hours	5.29
24 hrs	3 hours	6.55
	12 hours	9.73

*also at 165 and 150 West End

Monterey Garage	1 hour	$4.00
137 West 89th Street	2 hours	5.00
Columbus-Amsterdam Aves	max to 6 pm	7.00
	after 6 pm	1.00 per hr.

UPPER EAST SIDE

Regency Garage	1 hour	$5.07
239 E. 63rd Street (3-2 Aves)	2 hours	5.71
24 hrs.	up to midnight	9.73
	24 hours	12.26

Manhattan Parking System	any 12 hrs.	$ 8.46
202 East 67th Street		
Betw. 2nd & 3rd Aves		

(If you find yourself parking on a monthly basis you may be entitled to a tax exemption certificate. Contact:
NYC Dept of Finance, Parking Tax Exemption section,
25 Elm Street, Bklyn, NY 11201. Tel. 718-935-6694)

CAR WASHES

Carzapoppin
610 Broadway (Houston St.)   673-5115
124 Avenue of the Americas (Broome St)

East Side
1770 First Avenue (92nd St.)   722-2222

Under West Car Wash
638 West 47th Street (12th Ave.)   757-1141

CAR THEFT

Currently there are almost 2 million car owners in this city. For many, the automobile is the most expensive possession besides one's home. Car theft is the most far-reaching property crime in New York City. It's estimated that the average owner has to pay an additional $360 in insurance fees per year. As recently as 1994, there have been 94,525 reported car thefts in NYC. If you think that's bad, it's actually an improvement. Just consider the all-time high of 146,300 auto thefts which took place in 1990.

In most cases motor vehicles are stolen for their parts. They are then sold to individuals or *chop shops,* which are illegal operations that buy stolen cars.

NEW YORK FUN FACT

According to the NYPD, Queens has the most stolen cars in all of NYC. Flushing was first with 1700 car thefts in 1995. Second place went to Fresh Meadows, and in third was Queen Village. One theory offered is that the borough of Queens has many surrounding highways which offer quick escapes for thieves.

10 MOST LIKELY-TO-BE STOLEN CARS IN NYC

1. HONDA ACCORD
2. TOYOTA CAMRY
3. ACURA LEGEND
4.. NISSAN MAXIMA
5. HONDA CIVIC
6. TOYOTA COROLLA
7. OLDSMOBILE CUTLASS
8. LINCOLN TOWN CAR
9. FORD TAURUS
10. NISSAN SENTRA

Least Likely to be stolen: CHEVY LUMINA and SAAB 900

Source: Auto Crime Div. - NYPD

MOST DANGEROUS CARS ON THE ROAD

- ⊙ GO Tracker
- *Chevrolet Corvette
- Isuzu Amigo
- Hundai Scoupe
- Ford Mustang
- Isuzu Trooper
- Acura SLX

*Vehicles which carry the highest death rate between 1990-1994.
⊙ *Tracker's* death rate in roll-over crashes is more than 6 times the national average.

Top List of Lowest Death Vehicles

- Volvo 240
- Saab 9000
- Mercedes 190 DE

Large or mid size were safest. All but one carried air bags.
Source: The Insurance Institute for Highway Safety

 KEY NUMBERS

- *License Express*   645-5550
(to avoid long lines renewing your drivers license)
300 West 34th Street (Betw. 8-9 Aves.)

- *Parking Ticket Hotline*   477-4430

- *Ticket Fighters* (for commercial vehicles)   666-6514

#36   *"First you gotta get their attention!"*
Proverb

MAKING A BIG STINK

There used to be an expression from my boyhood days that I remember my grandfather using every time he was fuming mad about some dirty deal in city government. "Go fight City Hall", he used to say with a good deal of resignation in his voice. The message was that it was all hopeless.

Back in the 50's and early 60's there was no denying the fact that things *were* different. With few exceptions, people really didn't question authority. They did pretty much what they were told. Perhaps it was blind faith, perhaps it was out of reverence for those in power. A good many just bit their lip and carried on.

Not too many years later it dawned on people that they knew just as much if not more than those in positions of authority. It was the beginning of an awareness that shaped the social conscience of America. Citizens got to see those in power as being more than occasionally careless and corrupt. Certainly episodes such as Vietnam and Watergate unveiled a stark reality that we haven't recovered from yet.

On a local level, imagine if you will what would happen in our present social climate if the old Brooklyn Dodgers and New York Giants tried to abandon this city in much the same way as they did in 1957. Knowing what we know, I doubt very much if most folks today would just take it on the chin.

I'd be willing to bet that there would be an uproar the likes of which you've never seen.

"Many voices speak louder than one voice," says Stacy Sherman, Director of Communications for the Citizens Committee. The Committee is a privately-operated, not-for-profit organization which trains residents to organize block associations. "By organizing you're better able to capitalize on the different skills, resources and ideas of different people."

"If you have kids toting guns walking up and down your block -- I'm sure everybody would get involved in trying to do something about it," says Sherman. Sherman believes that people tend to organize around a problem. And in a lot of cases when that problem is solved, the group is not that active.

According to a study conducted by the U.S. Office of Consumer Affairs entitled, "Consumer Complaint Handling in America" nearly 70% of those consumers with problems don't complain. Most folks *won't* make waves which in turn causes those of us who do to work harder. *"Go fight City Hall"* translates into ' *Why bother? Nothing will be done anyway."* Perhaps that's why a very small percentage of crimes in the city are ever reported. However, if enough people know how to complain effectively and what buttons to push, the message resonates loud and clear.

Given enough complaints, changes are far more likely to occur. There's absolutely no good in biting the wall in frustration. Those close to you will be on the receiving end of your anger which serves no purpose at all. Your one letter might just be *the one* that breaks the camel's back. A friend of mine summed it up succinctly, "You have to feel that you can make a difference."

Even more effective is complaining as a group, even if it is only two or three. Organizing other folks who feel equally disgruntled about something can send a very powerful message. We all remember Peter Finch's immortal words in the movie *Network: "I want you all to rise out of your chair, go to the window and say I'm as mad as hell and I'm not going to take it anymore!"* Is it just coincidence that this scene took place in New York? I think not. New Yorkers are no strangers to complaining.

The Runaround and Stonewalling

The runaround occurs when a city agency or company switches you from extension to extension and departments are highly reluctant to take responsibility for a problem you might have. They may tell you they'll get back to you and they don't. If this has ever happened to you, you know how frustrating this can be. Going after the chain of command, whether it be the head of the department or the president of the company is often a strategy that proves effective.

It saves a good deal of time knowing that subordinates at municipal offices don't set policy or have the authority to deviate from it. When it comes to a city agency that is dragging its feet, one option I personally endorse is going directly to the Public Advocate's office (212-669-7200) or the Mayors Office of Operations (212-788-1467).

These offices act as liaisons, oversee all city agencies and often get results. Consider sending a copy of your complaint to the Borough President's office as a follow up. Don't be afraid of going directly to the Commissioner's office of a city agency if you find that their *Help Hotline* is not accessible, keeps you on hold forever or cuts you off. Chances are you are not the only one experiencing the problem.

ORGANIZING

Of all communities in New York City, one of the most active without a doubt is Bay Ridge, Brooklyn where there is always a petition being circulated. Bay Ridge has been termed "a model of grass roots activism where civic responsibility is openly praised and made contagious". This community has over 100 civic groups and has stopped the closing of Fort Hamilton, reduced 3-hour alternate side of the street parking to 90 minutes, blocked the opening of a MacDonalds and kept out high-rise buildings. The residents are also trying to block the opening of a United Aritst multiplex movie theater. "Bay Ridge is one such community that refuses to be pushed out to New Jersey or Staten Island" said one community activist.

Remember when a certain developer, who shall remain nameless, promised to erect the world's tallest building on the Upper West Side? The community fought back. *Coalition for a Livable West Side* and local residents stopped him from doing so. They along with Community Board # 7 forced him to modify an entire multi-million dollar project. Tenants organized, pooled their resources and pressured community boards and politicians to stop the mogul's plans from materializing. The world's tallest building will now have to built closer to the world's biggest ego.

Even our own FBI resorted to 'take no prisoner' tactics when they brought in huge loudspeakers, played irritating sounds, and tried to weaken the resistance of a religious cult in Waco, Texas some years ago. That particular maneuver did not prove successful, but it was an attempt to help bring the other side to the bargaining table.

If you're not the "organizing" type, then take more of an interest in your local block association, tenant group, and

local community board for starters. There is always more
strength in numbers. Even getting together with just a few of
your neighbors who share a common complaint will prove
beneficial.

GET A GRIP

- Contact your Senator, Council or Assemblyperson and
  speak up. Don't quit. The key to all of this is being
  persistent. If you're not satisfied with the way a city
  agency is handling your complaint contact the offices of
  Public Advocate and the Mayor's Office of Operations.

- The Public Advocate's staff can facilitate your complaint
  with city agencies and services. It is a watchdog office
  that is set up to reveal deficiencies with agencies and
  serves as a go between for citizens and government. The
  office fields about 10,000 complaints yearly.

The **Ombudsman Unit** *(originally a Swedish word meaning
"go-between")* accepts complaints daily Monday-Friday.

Public Advocate	Mayors Office of Operations
Mark Green	(troubleshoots city agencies)
1 Centre Street	Tyra Liebmann
Municipal Bldg.	100 Church Street
New York, NY 10007	New York, NY 10007
Tel. 662-7200	Tel. 788-1467
Fax 669-4701	Fax 788-1665

Finally, consider going to the press and making your
grievance public.

MAKING A BIG STINK

There's nothing like spreading the word when you feel like you've been wronged. News bureaus are also a good source. Local TV and radio stations have consumer affairs reporters who often take an interest in an unresolved complaint. No matter what anybody tries to tell you, remember, nine out of ten times there are things you can do to get satisfaction. You should also be familiar with your local legislators because they prove to be helpful more often than not. For a complete list of all NYC legislators see the end of this chapter.

KEEPING THE HEAT ON

GOING TO NEWS DESKS

News Desk	Telephone	Fax
ABC	456-7777	456-2381
NBC	664-4444	664-2994
CBS	975-4321	975-9387
FOX	452-3800	249-1182
WOR	201-348-0009	201-330-3844
WPIX	949-1100	210-2591
NY1	NY1-NEWS	563-7154
Daily News	210-NEWS	682-4953
NY Times	556-1234	556-3690
City Line	556-3800	556-7793

News Desk	*Telephone*	*Fax*
Post	930-8500	719-0824
Wall St. Journal	416-3131	416-3299
Newsday	718-575-2550	718-793-6422
Village Voice	475-3333	475-8944
Manhattan Spirit	268-8600	268-0503
New York Press	941-1130	941-7824
Our Town	268-8600	268-0503
The Resident	679-1850	679-4886
Downtown Express	242-6162	229-2790

WIRE SERVICES

Associated Press	621-1500	621-1679
United Press Intl.	560-1100	643-8970
Reuters	603-3401	486-1496

TV CONSUMER REPORTERS

☛ *Consumer Update*   NBC   765-4272
(Asa Aarons) News 4 NY   fax   664-6385
E-mail address: askasa@nbc.com

☛ *Eyewitness News*   ABC   456-3146
(Tappy Phillips)   fax   456-2381

☛ *"Steals & Deals"*   CNBC   201-585-6459
(John Donovan)   fax   201-585-6282

☛ *20/20*   ABC   456-2020
(Arnold Diaz)   fax   456-2969

(also consider the editorial desk of New York Magazine
reachable at 508-0783 - fax: 583-7516)

THE URBAN GUERRILLA

If you have a legitimate beef in your community and find yourself without a block association to lean on, all is not lost. Community activist and disgruntled New Yorker Harry Klein recommends inventing your own organization on paper.

Create a letterhead calling yourself a "Such and Such Street Neighborhood Coalition" or a "Community Alliance" or whatever. It carries more weight and is sure to make a more lasting impression. If you want to get a little fancier, rent a Post Office Box as the organization's mailing address.

YOUR NEW YORK ELECTED OFFICIALS

MANHATTAN

Council Districts

1 Kathryn E. Freed (D)   51 Chambers St.
NY 10007   788-7722   Fax 788-7727
2 Antonio Pagan (D-L)   237 First Ave.
NY 10003   477-1203   Fax 477-0776
3 Thomas K Duane (D-L)   275 7th Ave.
NY 10001   929-5501   Fax 929-5562
4 Andrew Eristoff (R)   409 E. 14th St.
NY 10009   473-4960   Fax 473-6295
5 Gifford A. Miller   336 E. 73rd St.
NY 10021   535-5554   Fax 535-6098
6 Ronnie Eldridge (D-L)   10 Columbus Cir.
NY 10019   765-4339   Fax 765-4805
7 Stanley Michels (D-L)   City Hall
NY 10007   788-7700   Fax 788-7712

8   Adam C Powell IV (D-L) 159 E.. 116th St
NY 10029   427-0700   Fax 427-7540
9   C. Virginia Fields (D-L) 163 W. 125th St
NY 10027   662-4440   Fax 932-1130
10 Guillermo Linares (D)   656 W. 181st St.
10033   781-0856   Fax 740-1573
22 Peter F. Vallone (D)   22-45 31st St. Astoria, 11105
718-274-4500   Fax 718-726-0357

State Senatorial Districts

25   Martin Connor (D-L)   270 Broadway
NY 10007   417-5512   Fax 964-5776
26   Roy Goodman (R-L)   270 Broadway
NY 10007   417-5563   Fax 417-5566
27   Catherine Abate (D)   270 Broadway
NY 10007   417-5504   Fax 964-4775
28   Olga Mendez (D-L)   2130 Third Ave.
NY 10035   860-0893   Fax 831-0530
29   David Paterson (D)   163 W. 125th St
NY 10027   961-8500   Fax 678-0001
30   Franz Leichter (D-L)   10 Columbus Circle
NY 10019   397-5913   Fax 397-3201

State Assembly Districts

62   Sheldon Silver (D-L)   270 Broadway
NY 10007   312-1420   Fax 312-1425
63   Steven Sanders (D-L)   201 E. 16th St
NY 10003   979-9696   Fax 979-0594
64   Richard Gottfried (D-L)   242 W. 27th St
NY 10001   807-7900   Fax 243-2035
65   Alexander Grannis (D-L) 1672 First Ave
NY 10128   860-4906   Fax 996-3046
66   Deborah Glick (D-L)   853 Broadway
NY 10003   674-5153   Fax 674-5530

67   Scott Stringer (D)   230 W. 72nd St
NY 10023   873-6368   Fax 873-6520
68   Nelson Denis (D)   (newly elected call 674-8484)
69   Edward Sullivan (D-L)   245 W. 104th St
NY 10025   866-3970   Fax 864-1095
70   Keith Wright (D)   163 W. 125th St
NY 10027   866-5809   Fax 864-1368
71   Herman Farrell (D-L)   2541-55 A. C. Powell Blvd.
NY 10039   234-1430   Fax 234-1868
72   Adriano Espaillat (D) (newly elected call 674-8484)
73   John Ravitz - (R)   251 E. 77th St
NY 10021   861-9061   Fax 861-5273

Congressional Districts

8 Jerrold Nadler (D-L)   11 Beach St
NY 10013   334-3207   Fax 334-5259
12 Nydia Velazquez (D)   815 Broadway
Bklyn 11206   718-599-3658 Fax 718-599-4537
14 Carolyn Maloney (D-L)   110 E. 59th St
NY 10022   832-6531   Fax 832-7576
15 Charles Rangel (D-L)   163 W. 125th St
NY 10027   663-3900   Fax 663-4277

BROOKLYN

33   Kenneth K. Fisher (D-L)   16 Court St.
Bklyn 11241   718-875-5200   Fax 718-643-6620
34   Victor L. Robles (D-L)   815 Broadway
Bklyn 11206   718-963-3141   Fax 718-963-4527
35   Mary Pinkett (D)   324 DeKalb Ave.
Bklyn 11205   718-857-0959   Fax 718-857-5524
36   Annette Robinson (D-L)   1360 Fulton St
Bklyn 11221   718-399-8900   Fax 718-399-6099
37   Martin Malave-Dilan (D)   786 Knickerbocker Ave
Bklyn 11207   718-453-4674   Fax 718-453-4727

38   Joan Griffin McCabe (D)   406 43rd St
Bklyn 11232   718-436-2215   Fax 718-436-2656
39   Stephen DiBrienza (D-L)   2902 Ft. Hamilton Pkwy
Bklyn 11218   718-435-9801   Fax 718-435-6591
40   Una Clarke (D)   648 New York Ave
Bklyn 11203   718-493-7065   Fax 718-493-8285
41   Enoch H. Williams (D)   1670 Fulton St.
Bklyn 11213   718-604-8132   Fax 718-953-2898
42   Priscilla A. Wooten (D-R)   1962 Linden Blvd
Bklyn 11207   718-272-3055   Fax 718-927-2584
43   Salvatore F. Albanese (D-L) 476 76th St
Bklyn 11209   718-748-4722   Fax 718-921-0366
44   Noach Dear (D-C)   4424 16th Ave
Bklyn 11230   718-633-9400   Fax 718-633-9403
45   Lloyd Henry (D-L)   1498 Flatbush Ave
Bklyn 11210   718-421-6621   Fax 718-421-6625
46   Herbert E. Berman (D-L)   250 Broadway
NYC   10007   212-788-6984
47   Howard L. Lasher (D-L)   2971 Ocean Pkwy
Bklyn 11235   718-646-5550   Fax 718-648-4240
48   Anthony David Weiner (D)   1901 Avenue U
Bklyn 11229   718-332-9001   Fax 718-332-9010
50   John A. Fusco (R-C)   94 Lincoln Ave
Staten Is. 10306   718-980-1017   Fax 718-980-1051

State Senate Districts

12   Ada L. Smith (D-L)   130-08 Rockaway Blvd
So. Ozone Pk 11420 718-322-2537   Fax 718-322-8417
17   Nellie Santiago (D-L)   545 Broadway
Bklyn   11206   718-782-6228   Fax 718-782-9185
18   Velmanette Montgomery (D)   70 Lafayette Ave
Bklyn   11217   718-643-6140   Fax   718-237-4137
19   Howard E. Babbush (D-L)   270 Broadway
NYC   10007   212-417-5517   Fax   212-964-8233

20   Marty Markowitz (D)   572 Flatbush Ave
Bklyn   11225   718-284-4700   Fax   718-282-3585
21   Carl Kruger (D-L)   2201 Avenue U
Bklyn   11229   718-743-8610   Fax   718-743-5958
22   Seymour Lachman (D)   2346 86th St
Bklyn   11214   718-449-1443   Fax   718-372-5749
23   Vincent J. Gentile (D) (newly elected call 674-8484)
25   Martin Connor (D-L)   270 Broadway
NYC   10007   212-417-5512   Fax   212-964-5776

State Assembly Districts

39   Anthony J. Genovesi (D)   270 Broadway
NYC   10007   212-385-6636   Fax   212-385-6639
40   Edward Griffith (D-L)   270 Broadway
NYC   10007   212-385-6696   Fax   212-385-6687
41   Helene E. Weinstein (D-L)   3520 Nostrand Ave
Bklyn   11229   718-648-4700
42   Rhonda S. Jacobs (D-L)   3 Hillel Place
Bklyn   11210   718-434-0446   Fax   718-421-4396
43   Clarence Norman, Jr. (D-L)   854 Nostrand Ave
Bklyn   11225   718-756-1776   Fax   718-778-3010
44   James F. Brennan (D-L)   416 Seventh Ave
Bklyn   11215   718-788-7221   Fax   718-965-9378
45   Daniel L. Feldman   (D)   1227 Avenue U
Bklyn   11229   718-375-0770   Fax   718-376-8028
46   Jules Polonetsky (D-L)   532 Neptune Ave
Bklyn   11224   718-265-6530   Fax   718-265-6537
47   William Colton (newly elected - call 212-674-8484)
48   Dov Hikind (D-R-C)   1310 48th St
Bklyn   11219   718-853-0606   Fax   718-436-5734
49   Peter J. Abbate, Jr. (D)   8500 18th Ave
Bklyn   11214   718-236-1764   Fax   718-234-0986
50   Joseph R. Lentol (D)   619 Lorimer St
Bklyn   11211   718-383-7474   Fax 718-383-1576

51   Felix W. Ortiz (D)   404 55th St
Bklyn   11220   718-492-6334   Fax 718-492-6435
52   Eileen C. Dugan (D-L)   343 Smith St
Bklyn   11231   718-875-2311   718-237-5908
53   Vito J. Lopez (D-L)   1438 Myrtle Ave
Bklyn   11237   718-452-1112   718-452-7057
54   Darryl C. Towns (D)   264 Jamaica Ave
Bklyn   11207   718-235-5627   718-235-5966
55   William F. Boyland (D-L)   1636 Pitkin Ave
Bklyn   11212   718-498-8681   718-498-8807
56   Albert Vann (D)   613 Throop Ave
Bklyn   11216   718-919-0740   718-919-0744
57   Roger L. Green (D)   55 Hanson Place
Bklyn   11217   718-596-0100   718-834-0865
58   N. Nick Perry (D-L)   942 Utica Ave
Bklyn   11203   718-385-3336   718-385-3339

Congressional Districts

8   Jerrold L. Nadler (D-L)   11 Beach St
NY   10013   212-334-3207   Fax 212-334-5259
9   Charles E. Schumer (D-L)   1628 Kings Hwy
Bklyn   11229   718-627-9700   Fax 718-627-3411
10   Edolphus Towns (D-L)   545 Broadway
Bklyn   11206   718-387-8696   Fax 718-387-8045
11   Major R. Owens (D-L)   289 Utica Ave
Bklyn   11213   718-773-3100   Fax 718-735-7143
12   Nydia M. Velazquez (D-L)   815 Broadway
Bklyn   11206   718-599-3658   Fax 718-599-4537
13   Susan Molinari (R-C)   14 New Dorp Lane
Staten Island 10306 718-987-8400   Fax 718-987-8938
14   Carolyn B. Maloney (D)   110 E. 59th St
NY   10022   212-832-6531   Fax 212-832-7576

BRONX

Council Districts

8	Adam C. Powell (D-L)	159 E. 116th St
NY 10029	212-427-0700	Fax 212-427-7540
11	June M. Eisland (D-L)	3636 Waldo Ave
Bronx 10463	718-549-0158	
12	Lawrence A. Warden (D-L)	657 E 233rd St
Bronx 10466	718-884-9951	Fax 718-884-9956
13	Michael DeMarco (D-C)	80 Westchester Sq
Bronx 10461	718-931-6063	Fax 718-518-8443
14	Israel Ruiz, Jr. (D-L)	1 E. Fordham Rd
Bronx 10468	718-220-0738	Fax 718-220-0721
15	Jose Rivera (D-L)	2488 Grand Concourse
Bronx 10458	718-364-3700	Fax 718-365-5267
16	Wendell Foster (D-L)	1377 Jerome Ave
Bronx 10452	718-588-7500	Fax 718-588-7790
17	David Rosado (D-L)	558 Melrose Ave
Bronx 10455	718-402-7602	Fax 718-402-7735
18	Lucy Cruz (D-L)	1967 Turnbull Ave
Bronx 10473	718-518-7110	Fax 718-518-7016
22	Peter F. Vallone	22-45 31st St
Astoria 11105	718-274-4500	Fax 718-726-0357

State Senate Districts

28	Olga A. Mendez (D-L-R)	2130 Third Ave
NY 10035	212-860-0893	Fax 212-831-0530
30	Franz S. Leichter (D-L)	10 Columbus Cir
NY 10019	212-397-5913	Fax 212-397-3201
31	Efrain Gonzalez, Jr. (D)	1780 Grand Concourse
Bronx 10457	718-299-7905	Fax 718-583-8249
32	David Rosado (D) (newly elected call 674-8484)	
33	Larry B. Seabrook (D)	3677 White Plains
Bronx 10467	718-547-8854	Fax 718-515-2718

34   Guy J. Velella (R-C-D)   2019 Williamsbrdg
Bronx 10461 718-792-7180   Fax 718-792-3924

Congressional Districts

7   Thomas J. Manton (D)   46-12 Queens Blvd
Sunnyside 11104 718-706-1400   Fax 718-472-0489
15   Charles B. Rangel (D-L)   163 W. 125th St
NY 10027   718-663-3900   Fax 718-663-4277
16   Jose E. Serrano (D-L)   890 Grand Concourse
Bronx 10451   718-538-5400   Fax 718-588-3652
17   Eliot L. Engel (D-L)   3655 Johnson Ave
Bronx 10463   718-796-9700   Fax 718-796-5134
18   Nita Lowey (D)   97-45 Queens Blvd
Rego Park 11374 718-897-3602   Fax 718-897-3804

State Assembly Districts

74   Carmen E. Arroyo (D-R-L)   384 E. 149th St
Bronx 10455 718-292-2901   Fax 718-292-6021
75   Ruben Diaz (D)   (newly elected call 212-674-8484)
76   Peter M. Rivera (D-L)   1916 Benedict Ave
Bronx 10462 718-931-2620   Fax 718-931-2915
77   Aurelia Greene (D-L)   1188 Grand Concourse
Bronx   10456 718-538-2000   Fax 718-538-3310
78   Roberto Ramirez (D-L)   2488 Grand Concourse
Bronx   10458 718-933-2204   Fax 718-933-2535
79   Gloria Davis (D)   540 E. 169th St
Bronx   10456 718-588-3119   Fax 718-588-3317
80   Jeffrey Klein (D)   728 Lydig Ave
Bronx   10462 718-409-0109
81   Jeffrey Dinowitz (D-L)   3107 Kingsbridge
Bronx   10463 718-796-5345   Fax 718-796-0694
82   Stephen B. Kaufman (D-C)   2910 Bruckner Ave
Bronx   10465 718-829-7452   Fax 718-597-5037

83   Larry B. Seabrook (D)   3677 White Plains
Bronx 10467 718-547-8854   Fax 718-515-2718

QUEENS

Council Districts

19   Michael J. Abel (R-C)   199-17A 32 Ave
Bayside 11358 718-352-0200   Fax 718-352-5405
20   Julia Harrison (D-L)   39-15 Main St
Flushing 11354 718-886-7040   Fax 718-359-4973
21   Helen M. Marshall (D-L)   97-19 Astoria Blvd
Elmhurst 11369 718-507-0813   Fax 718-507-1840
22   Peter F. Vallone   22-45 31st St
Astoria 11105 718-274-4500   Fax 718-726-0357
23   Sheldon S. Leffler (D-L)   205-07 Hillside Av
Hollis   11423 718-465-8202   Fax 718-776-2302
24   Morton Povman (D)   108-18 Queens Blvd
Forest Hills 11375 718-793-2255   Fax 718-268-3499
25   John D. Sabini (D)   37-32 75th St
Jackson Hts 11372 718-507-3688   Fax 718-507-2982
26   Walter L. McCaffrey (D-R-L)   62-07 Woodside Ave
Woodside   11377 718-639-1400
27   Archie Spigner (D-L)   113-39 Farmer's Mkt
St. Albans   11412 718-776-3700   Fax 718-776-3798
28   Thomas White, Jr. (D-L)   146-01 Rockaway Blvd
Jamacia   11436 718-322-6121   Fax 718-322-6125
29   Karen Koslowitz (D)   118-21 Queens Blvd
Forest Hills 11375 718-544-3212   Fax 718-261-5022
30   Thomas V. Ognibene (R-C)   78-25 Metropolitan Ave
Middle Village 11379 718-366-3900   Fax 718-326-3549
31   Juanita E. Watkins (D-L)   220-07 Merrick Blvd
Laurelton 11413   718-527-4356   Fax 718-527-4402
32   Alfonso Stabile (R-C)   105-20 Cross bay Blvd
Ozone Park 11417 718- 843-5283   Fax 718-843-5561

State Senate Districts

10 Alton R. Waldon, Jr. (D-L)	172-12 Linden Blvd
St. Albans 11434 718-291-9097	Fax 718-291-9398
11 Frank Padavan (R-C)	89-39 Gettysburg St
Bellrose, 11426 718-343-0255	Fax 718-343-0354
12 Ada L. Smith (D-L)	130-08 Rockaway Blvd
So. Ozone Park 11420 718-322-2537	Fax 718-322-8417
13 Emanuel R. Gold (D-L)	70-17 Austin St
Forest Hills 11375 718-544-9750	Fax 718-261-1179
14 George Onorato (D)	28-11 Astoria Blvd
Astoria 11102 718-545-9706	Fax 718-726-2036
15 Serphin R. Maltese (R-C)	71-04 Myrtle Ave
Glendale 11385 718-497-1800	Fax 718-386-7803
16 Leonard P. Stavisky (D-L)	144-36 Willets Pt Blvd
Flushing 11357 718-445-0004	Fax 718-445-8398

Congressional Districts

5 Gary L. Ackerman (D-L)	218-14 Northern Blvd
Bayside 11361 718-423-2154	Fax 718-423-5053
6 Floyd H. Flake (D)	196-06 Linden Blvd
St. Albans 11412 718-949-5600	Fax 718-949-5972
7 Thomas J. Manton (D)	46-12 Queens Blvd
Sunnyside 11104 718-706-1400	Fax 718-472-0489
9 Charles E. Schumer (D-L)	1628 Kings Hwy
Bklyn 11229 718-627-9700	Fax 718-627-3411
12 Nydia M. Velazquez (D-L))	815 Broadway
Bklyn 11206 718-599-3658	Fax 718-599-4537
14 Carolyn B. Maloney (D)	110 E. 59th St
NY 10022 212-832-6531	Fax 212-832-7576
15 Charles B. Rangel (D-L)	163 W. 125th St
NY 10027 718-663-3900	Fax 718-663-4277
18 Nita Lowey (D)	97-45 Queens Blvd
Rego Park 11374 718-897-3602	Fax 718-897-3804

State Assembly Districts

23   Audrey I. Pheffer (D-L)   90-16 Rockaway Beach Blvd
Rockaway Beach 718-945-9550   Fax 718-945-9549
24   Mark Weprin (D-L)   61-08A 224th St
Bayside 11364   718-428-7900   Fax 718-428-8575
25   Brian M. McLaughlin (D-L) 35-20 147th St
Flushing 11354   718-762-6575   Fax 718-762-0917
26   Ann Margaret Carrozza (newly elected call 674-8484)
27   Nettie Mayersohn (D-L)   65-01 Fresh Meadow Lane
Flushing 11365   718-463-1942   Fax 718-358-1979
28   Melinda Katz (D-L)   98-08 Metropolitan Ave
Forest Hills 11375 718-263-5595 Fax 718-263-5688
29   William Scarborough (D-L) 119-02 Merrick Blvd
St. Albans 11434   718-949-5216   Fax 718-949-5275
30   Joseph Crowley (D)   84-32 Grand Ave
Elmhurst 11373   718-651-3185   Fax 718-651-3027
31   Gregory W. Meeks (D-L)   21-17 Mott Ave
Far Rockaway 11691 718-337-4343 Fax 718-337-2627
32   Vivian E. Cook (D-L)   142-15 Rockaway Blvd
Jamacia 11436 718-322-3975   Fax 718-322-4085
33   Barbara M. Clark (D-L)   97-01 Springfield Blvd
Queens Village 11429 718-479-2333 Fax 718-464-7128
34   Ivan C. Lafayette (D-L)   33-46 92nd St
Jackson Heights 11372 718-457-0384 Fax 718-335-8254
35   Jeffrion L. Aubry (D-L)   102-13A Northern Blvd
Corona 11368 718-457-3615   Fax 718-457-3640
36   Denis J. Butler (D)   43-08 30th Ave
LIC 11103 718-932-4052   Fax 718-932-4176
37   Catherine T. Nolan (D)   879 Woodward Ave
Ridgewood 11385 718-456-9492   Fax 718-417-4982
38   Anthony S. Seminerio (D)   114-19 Jamacia Ave
Richmond Hill 11418 718-847-0770 Fax 718-847-9346

STATEN ISLAND

Council Districts

49   Jerome X. O'Donovan (D-C)   36 Richmond Terr
Staten Isl 718-727-9730   Fax 718-816-8407
50   John A. Fusco (R-C)   94 Lincoln Ave
Staten Isl 718-980-1017   Fax 718-980-1051
51   Vito J. Fossella, Jr. (R-C)   3944 Richmond Ave
Staten Isl 718-984-5151   Fax 718-984-5737

State Senate Districts

23   Vincent J. Gentile (D) (newly elected call 674-8484)
24   John J. Marchi (D-R-L)   358 St. Marks Pl
Staten Isl 10301 718-447-1723   Fax 718-981-1270

Congressional District

13   Susan Molinari (R-C)   14 New Dorp Lane
Staten Isl 10306   718-987-8400   Fax 718-987-8938
(all of Staten Island)

State Assembly Districts

59   Elizabeth A. Connelly (D)   1150 Forest Hill Rd
Staten Isl 10314   718-494-3200   Fax 718-983-5620
60   Eric N. Vitaliano (D-C)   1736 Richmond Ave
Staten Isl   10314   718-761-5083   Fax 718-698-7578
61   Robert A. Straniere (R-C)   182 Rose Ave Staten
Isl   10306   718-667-0314   Fax 718-987-4593

NYC LEGISLATORS WITH THE WORST
ATTENDANCE RECORDS

SENATE

1. Senator Pedro Espada *(D-Bronx)
2. Senator Martin Solomon** (D-Brooklyn)
3. Senator Howard Babbush (D-Brooklyn)
4. Senator Emanuel Gold (D-Queens)
5. Senator Leonard Stavisky (D-Queens)
6. Senator Nellie Santiago (D-Brooklyn)

ASSEMBLY

1. Assemblyman Dov Hikind (D-Brooklyn)
2. Assemblyman Frank Babaro (D-Brooklyn)
3. Assemblyman Anthony Genovesi (D-Brooklyn)
4. Assemblyman Albert Vann (D-Brooklyn)
5. Assemblyman Roger Green (D-Brooklyn)

---

* defeated in the November 1996 election
** resigned to become a civil court judge

Source: NYS Senate & Assembly - 1995-6 legislative term

BORO PRESIDENTS

Manhattan: Ruth W Messinger (D/L)
669-8300   Fax   669-4900
One Centre Street, Municipal Bldg., NYC 10007

Brooklyn: Howard Golden (D)
718-802-3700   Fax   718-802-3959
209 Joralemon St., Bklyn, NY 11201

Bronx: Fernando Ferrer (D)
718-590-3500   Fax   718-590-3537
851 Grand Concourse, Bronx, NY 10451

Queens: Claire Shulman (D)
718-286-2870   Fax   718-286-2885
120-55 Queens Blvd.,
Kew Gardens, NY   11424

Staten Island: Guy Molinari (R/C)
718-816-2200   Fax   718-816-2026
Borough Hall, Staten Isl, NY 10301

Mayor Rudolph Giuliani (R-L)
City Hall, New York, NY 10007
788-9600

Daniel P. Moynihan (D)   Alphonse M. D'Amato (R)
405 Lexington Avenue   7 Penn Plaza
New York, NY 10174   New York, NY 10001
661-5150   947-7390

Governor George Pataki (R)
633 Third Avenue
New York, NY 10017
681-4500

For up to the minute changes, contact:
The League of Women Voters, 817 Broadway,
NYC, 10003   677-5050 • Fax 677-5380

KEY NUMBERS

• *Citizens Committee for New York*   989-0909
Organizing block associations
grants, grass roots training

• *Mayor's Office of Operations*   788-1467
(If you're not getting satisfaction with a city agency)

• *Mayor's Office - Community Assistance*   788-7453

• *NYC Board Of Elections*   1-800-VOTE-NY

PART FIVE

I REALLY DO LOVE
THIS CITY

#37

12 BEST-KEPT SECRET ESCAPES
WHERE YOU CAN
GET AWAY FROM IT ALL

(FOR CLOSE TO NOTHING)

1. **WAVE HILL**
675 West 252 Street, Bronx 718-549-3200

Just a stones throw from Manhattan, (roughly 15 minutes), this country estate of 28 acres rests in the Riverdale section of the Bronx. Filled with glorious gardens, greenhouses, sweeping lawns, a gazebo in the wild garden and a lily pond. Mark Twain once leased Wave Hill back in 1901 and set up his own treehouse parlor in the branches of a chestnut. The woodlands are on a hill overlooking the Hudson. The view of the Palisades remains one of the breathtaking sites to behold. Other former owners include: Teddy Roosevelt and Arturo Toscanini.

Wave Hill is located at Independence Avenue and West 249th Street in the Riverdale section of the Bronx.
By subway: Take the #1 train to 231 Street Station. Transfer for the # 7 or # 10 bus to 252nd Street. Walk to 249th.
Metro North: to Riverdale Station.

2. **THE SOUTH COVE**
Battery Park City

A stroll down the esplanade at Liberty Street and you're hugging the banks of the Hudson River. Watch gentle waves hit the shore, towering seagulls and sweeping landscapes of Lady Liberty and Ellis Island. You'll swear Jersey and Brooklyn never looked so inviting.

Sailboats drift by while joggers and those on their lunch hour make use of the noonday sun. Walk a little further, and soon you'll be upon South Cove.

A serene hideaway alongside lilac and ivory rose bushes, floating dragonflies in summer where winding paths lead the way to this furthermost shore of Battery Park City. Once here, you overlook the Hudson from Pier A with little or no sign of snarling traffic jams or distraught minds bumping into one another. The World Trade Center is off in the distance to the north. It might as well be a hundred miles away.

South Cove is a delightful spot to escape to just below West Thames Street slightly due west of South End avenue. It's a splendid walk where you can take pictures or listen to your Walkman while you unwind from whatever ails you. Admission: free

By bus: Take the M10 bus south to Battery Park City and walk southwest to the Esplanade.

By subway: C or E train to Chambers Street and cross over West Street To Battery Park City.

3. MUSEUM OF TELEVISION AND RADIO

25 West 52nd Street, bet. Fifth and Avenue of Americas

This retreat in midtown provides a wondrous escape to an inexhaustible collection of news and entertainment programs from years past. There are five floors filled with exhibits, screenings, seminars and private viewing of just about any radio and television program on file.

Founded by William S. Paley in 1975, this all-embracing collection of more than 60,000 programs includes documentaries, comedies, commercials, sports, children's shows, news, and the performing arts. Settle back in the private viewing room on the third floor and be magically transported back to the images and events that you fondly recall. Seeing them again is like seeing an old childhood friend.

By bus: M1, 2, 3, 4 bus to 52nd and Fifth Avenue.

By subway: R or N train to 53rd Street. Admission: by contribution.

4. THE HEATHER GARDEN

Fort Tryon Park, Cabrini Plaza and Margaret Corbin Plaza.

At the furthermost northern end of Manhattan island you'll find three parks all within close proximity to one another. Inwood Park, Isham Park, and Fort Tryon's sprawling woodlands make it hard to believe that these glorious hills and valleys are all part of Manhattan.

Besides being one of the largest heather and heath gardens on the East Coast (600 feet in length), there is something almost always in bloom year round. The heaths and spring bulbs begin flowering early in January and February.

Sweeping views of the George Washington Bridge, The Palisades and Hudson River are 240 feet below. Despite budget cuts, the Parks department has made a commitment to keep the Heather Garden one of the loveliest retreats available. The Cloisters Museum is just a five minute walk down the road.

By Bus: The M4 to Cabrini Blvd. - Margaret Corbin Plaza.
By subway: A train to 190th Street Overlook Terrace.

5. SONY WONDER
550 Madison Avenue, between 55th & 56th Sts

This unique, relatively new addition to New York allows one to escape to an electronic sanctuary of switches, screens, and commands all at your fingertips. If after being ignored in the big city you want to turn things around, this is the place.

Your adventure begins on the futuristic elevator which transports you to a room that resembles outer space with small beams of light looking like thousands of distant stars. Next it's onto the check-in station where you have your voice and picture recorded on an identity card. This serves as your passport to the rest of the exhibition where the main computer records your experiences.

Different activities await you, including a paint station that's made up of a giant wand that paints images on a computer screen. Touch sensitive displays and professional studios where you can try your hand at putting together a TV show, edit a music video and maneuver robots. Environmental crises and medical emergencies are simulated New York scenarios where visitors can control scientific research and robots at work stations. All in all there are 38 exhibits to choose from.

The high definition interactive theater, the only one of it's kind in New York City, allows visitors to navigate through a short film on technology. A joystick is connected to your seat. You can even help put together a new video game. The Sony Wonder allows you to have the opportunity to immerse yourself completely in mind-boggling electronic technology. Open Tues. & Fri., 10 am-9 p.m. Wed, Thurs., Sat, 10 am-6 p.m. Sunday 12 p.m.-6 p.m. Closed Monday. Admission free.
By bus: M1, 2, 3, 4 to Madison Avenue at 55th Street.
By subway: Take B train to 7th Ave station walk east 3 blocks to Madison Avenue

6. FLOWER GARDEN
Riverside Park, 91st Street and Riverside Drive

If it's beautiful seclusion you're after, The Flower Garden located on the double promenade past the children's playground in Riverside Park might be just what the doctor ordered. With a burst of bright yellows, reds, blues, purples, pinks and oranges, this haven is a great place for lunch, talking to friends, or just plain snoozing. Don't let the sounds of cars whizzing by down below from the Henry Hudson Parkway throw you. Before long, it won't even phase you as you overlook the 79th Street Boat Basin, a short walk away.

Here you'll behold over 50 different species of plants among 25 individual and diverse plots of land. Everything from trumpet vines, dahlias, hibiscus plants 12" wide and over 40 varieties of irises.

Park benches flank either side of the garden beneath towering trees. Run by a group called "The Garden People", the Flower Garden remains one of the sequestered havens in all of the city.
By bus: M5 bus to Riverside Drive and 91st Street. Walk to the downhill pathway past the Children's Playground. By subway: #1 train to 86th St. Short walk northwest.

7. BARNES & NOBLES BOOKSTORE
West 82nd Street & Broadway

With almost over a quarter of a million books and more than 1,000 newspapers and magazines at your disposal, this store is an oasis on the Upper West Side to escape to. You don't have to be "the book lover," to appreciate this haven far removed from the pressures of the city.

This store is more like a library to get delightfully lost in. Make no mistake about it, this is not just another bookstore. Here you can browse to your heart's content -- in fact it is actually welcomed. Voluminous levels of books surround the numerous shaker-style tables. Plush sofas and upholstered chairs (if you can find an empty one) for you to plop down in while escaping all the noise and insanity of the streets.

On the mezzanine level there is a cafe where you can take time out and order an exotic coffee, tea, or cool drink. A staff of about 120 sales folk are positioned throughout the store to assist you with your literary inquiries.

It is entirely conceivable to spend the entire day here if you choose to do so -- you'll be all the more likely to dream

on. Guest authors give free lectures regularly. Barnes &
Noble is located at Broadway and West 82nd Street. Their
downtown counterpart is at 21st Street and Avenue of the
Americas.
By bus: The M104 bus
*By subway: Take #1 train to 79th Street and walk 2 blocks
north.*

8. **PALEY PARK**
East 53rd Street between Madison and Fifth Avenues

Even though Paley Park is not a park with rolling hills it
possesses a 20-foot waterfall which cascades 1800 gallons of
water per minute. 17 locust trees stand tall and, in place of
benches, individual chairs with tables adorn the park.

The best place to sit is close to the waterfall. You'll
experience a sense of calm where the deadening sounds of
the rat race are drowned out to not even a whisper. You may
also get a cool drink when relaxing at the refreshment stand
on the premises.

In the midst of midtown Manhattan, situated between
hotels, offices, and museums, Paley Park's busiest time is
the lunch hour, 12-2, which you should avoid. Paley Park
opens at 8 a.m. and closes at 8 p.m. seven days a week. Not
open in January or on national holidays. Admission: free.
*By bus: M1, 2, 3, 4 bus on either Fifth or Madison Aves to
53rd St.*
By subway: E or F to 53rd St.

9. **THE FORD FOUNDATION**
42nd Street, between First and Second Avenues

One block west of the United Nations building, this temperate garden landscape has won all kinds of national awards. Its glass wall stands at 160 feet high and encloses one of the most desirable getaways for peace and quiet. The Ford Foundation opened in 1967 and is one of the most peaceful spots in the city. Here, you'll find over 20,000 varieties of vegetation and vines such as the eucalyptus plant and camellias which are not common to any other atrium in the country. There are over 20 different varieties of trees -- including weeping figs, a black olive tree, and a luxurious 18 ft Norfolk Island Pine.

There are three levels to this garden paradise with a water structure and small pond. You may make a wish and throw in a coin. All contributions go to UNICEF children's fund at the United Nations
By bus: M104 or M42 bus to 42nd Street & 2nd Ave
By subway: Any train to Grand Central Station

10. **CARL SCHURZ PARK**
East End Avenue and 85th Street

I bet if you asked a good many New Yorkers where Carl Schurz Park was, they wouldn't be able to tell you. That in my estimation makes this out of the way refuge a great hideaway.

Schurz Park houses Gracie Mansion, the mayor's official residence. The mansion is one of the oldest houses, built during the Revolutionary war, (late 1700's). The promenade known as John Finley Walk offers all-encompassing views of the East River, Roosevelt and Randall Islands. Ostentatious yachts and speed boats can be seen hot-dogging the waves.

The park is made up of more than 14 acres and runs as far north as 90th Street and south to east 83rd Street. Finley Walk continues onward to 81st Street and then winds down to a walkway beside the river that continues past where the Redwing tugboat docks. If you keep walking alongside the FDR drive, you'll pass a series of chess tables, a jogging station, and come to a pedestrian bridge at 63rd street that ends your journey by the shore.

At night the view of the Triborough Bridge all lit up is quite a sight to behold under the stars. Admission free.
By bus: 86th Street cross-town bus to East End Avenue and walk east a few steps.
By subway: 4,5,6 to 86th Street.

11. **STRAWBERRY FIELDS**
72nd Street and Central Park West

This teardrop shaped landscape is dedicated to the memory of John Lennon. Here you can sit amongst 3 bountiful acres and a lush stand of evergreen trees while eating lunch, listening to music, or just sitting back and people watching. Not only will your tortured New York digestive system unwind, but you'll find the air and the cared for surroundings conducive to clear thinking.   Relax amongst cobblestone-edged paths that lead through a circular garden.

Your dog, cat, or cockatoo is also welcome to take part in the shade. Just in case you want to bring your own picnic basket in the summer or take a friendly stroll, you may do so among the winding paths, tree clusters, and rock outcroppings.

On the ground near the entrance is a black and white marble mosaic, a gift of the city of Naples, Italy that bears the name "Imagine" from the title song by John Lennon celebrating peace and brotherhood. Over 100 countries have donated plants to Strawberry Fields.

By bus: M10 bus will bring you to the entrance of the park.
By subway: Take the B or C line to 72nd Street.

12. THE CONSERVATORY GARDEN
Fifth Avenue and 105th Street

I was surprised to learn that a good many New Yorkers have absolutely no knowledge of where or what this paradise is all about even though it can be found in their own backyard. Enter these 6 magical acres in Central Park and you'll be transported into another era.

You enter through towering wrought-iron gates that once stood as part of the Vanderbilt mansion at 58th Street and Fifth Avenue before it was demolished.

Complete with roses, wildflowers, and a spectrum of beautiful plants and foliage, the gardens make this a favorite site for weddings and other functions.

"Quiet zone in New York City" seems to be yet another one of those goofy oxymorons. The Conservatory Garden happens to be one of the few designated areas in all of Manhattan where you can hear yourself think. It remains New York's only formal garden.

Whether it's a stroll near several ornate fountains (one bearing water lilies and goldfish), The Secret Garden, crabapple allees, or one remarkable pergola complete with hanging vines, you'll be swept away by the serene beauty all gently nestled away.

You may rest on one of the benches that were designed for the 1939 World's Fair. The colors here are breathtakingly beautiful. Open everyday 8 am to dusk. Admission Free.
By bus: M1, 2, 3, 4 bus to 105th Street and Fifth Avenue.
By subway: # 6 train to 96th Street.

#38

HOW TO FIND AN APARTMENT IN NEW YORK *WITHOUT* A FEE

Regardless of how the average New Yorker complains, curses, and wishes him or herself out of here, there are hundreds who would gladly take his or her place. Everybody wants to make New York City their home these days, so it is no surprise that the vacancy rate is at a rock-bottom 1%.

Seems as though the only ones really benefiting are real estate brokers whose job it is to make sure you've got the bucks to buy your way into Manhattan. Next comes collecting a hefty commission (usually 15% of your yearly rent is their fee).

There's no doubt about it, looking for an apartment in the city is a time-consuming, frustrating and totally under-whelming experience. But if you have the persistence, you can save yourself a hefty fee with management companies that charge no commission.

Management companies are ensconced throughout the city but you must know just where to look. The hard part of locating these companies has already been done for you.

The companies listed in this chapter have access to apartments all around New York City, primarily in Manhattan. You have a fairly good shot at landing an apartment if you pursue these companies regularly with tact, good manners, and a sense of humor. The way you come across on the phone is very often the difference between landing an apartment and the phrase none of us want to hear, "nothing's available." It helps to be courteous so that this avenue remains a viable option for others as well.

With a little persistence you could save yourself a bundle! It beats perusing the obituary column for clues about recent vacancies.

WHAT TO EXPECT...

☞ You'll be asked what you're willing to spend a month and when you're looking to move. What size apartment you're looking for; (i.e. studio, 1 bedroom, etc.)

☞ If at first there is very little available to your liking, ask if it's okay to check back and the best time to do so. Very few want to be bothered with a waiting list or spending the day on the phone when having the apartment listed with an agent is a lot less time-consuming.

☞ Ask how often apartment lists are updated.

☞ Call at the middle and end of the month since many leases expire at those times.

BE PREPARED

○ Above all make sure you have an updated credit report.

○ If your credit is not on firm ground -- wait until you're asked to supply it.

○ It helps to have a letter from your current employer stating your time on the job and your current salary. Usually anyone answering the phone at your job can vouch for how long you've been there.

○ If you're in good standing with your present landlord be sure to have a letter stating that. If you're not, list friends or your folks as a prior address.

The following management companies *do not* charge a fee for their apartments. However a good many require a "credit check" fee. Those rates range anywhere from $0 to $200.

No Fee Management Companies

Solil Mgmt. Corp.
640 Fifth Avenue
New York, NY 10019
265-1667-8

Algin Mgmt Co.
64-35 Yellowstone Blvd.
Forest Hills, NY 11375
718-896-9600

Bettina Equities Co.
227 E. 85th Street
New York, NY 10028
744-3330

Building Mgmt Corp
52 Vanderbilt Ave
New York, NY 10017
557-6700

Fannie Klein
1641 First Ave
New York, NY 10028
570-6174

Rudin Mgmt Inc.
345 Park Avenue
New York, NY 10154
407-2400

Solow Building Co.
265 E. 66th St
New York, NY 10021
249-0303

Pine Mgmt Inc.
78 Manhattan Ave
New York, NY 10025
316-2114

B & L Management
344 E 63 St
New York, NY 10021
980-0980

Eberhart Brothers
312 East 82th Street
New York, NY 10028
570-2400

Bldg. Management
52 Vanderbilt Ave
New York, NY 10017
557-6700

Douglas Durst
1133 Ave of Americas
New York, NY 10036
789-1133

Brusco Mgmt.
163 West 74th Street
New York, NY 10023
595-9590

Whitehall Partners
250 W 100th Street
New York, NY 10025
222-9009

GFC Mgmt.
50 Broadway
New York, NY 10004
344-1444

Glenwood Mgmt
1440 York Avenue
New York, NY 10162
535-0500

William Gottlieb
544 Hudson Street
New York, NY 10014
989-3100

Philip Brodsky
188 Ave of Americas
New York, NY 10013
219-3990

Gamo Realty
826 Ninth Ave
New York, NY 10019
974-2187

Central Park Realty
221 W. 79th Street
New York, NY 10024
873-8100

Vifast Realty
122 W. 81st Street
New York, NY 10024
787-3487

Townhouse Mgmt Co.
432 E. 87th Street
New York, NY 10028
722-3313

Kinsey Company
163 West 23rd Street
New York, NY 10011
255-3579

Time Equities Inc.
55 Fifth Avenue
New York, NY 10022
206-6033

Manhattan Skyline
103 W. 55th Street
New York, NY 10019
889-1850

Shapolsky Mgmt.
608 East 11th Street
New York, NY 10009
228-1200

Cooper Square Realty
6 East 43rd St.
New York, NY 10017
682-7373

Kreisel Mgmt Co.
331 Madison Avenue
New York,, NY 10017
370-9200

Weinreb Management
276 Riverside Drive
New York, NY 10025
316-0045

Marin Mangement
463 Seventh Ave
New York, NY 10018
213-0123

MORE MANAGEMENT COMPANIES

- Related Companies   346-7900
- Grenadier Realty   595-6972
- 245-259 Realty Co.   243-7700
- Macklowe Corp.   988-5551
- Rockrose Development Corp.   557-3705
- Orb Mgmt   675-2680
- Abington Trust   759-5000
- 65 8th Ave Company   243-7700
- McAlpin Associates   736-0054
- 990 Avamericas Corp.   947-6200
- S-C Associates   582-4000
- Sherwood Equitties   980-8000
- Ansonia Associates   877-9800
- 304 W. 92nd Street Assoc   874-6000
- Rose Associates   316-1000
- Interstate Mgmt   316-4410
- Habitations   675-2680

- Milford Mgmt   753-7900
- Linmar L.P.   759-5000

OTHER SOURCES WORTH EXPLORING

✓ Apartment Fone   278-3663
   (free service, 24 hrs. Listings are read to you or faxed. Some listings come with brokers.)
✓ Apartment Source   343-8155
   (Service charges you $145. Listings via fax or e-mail: apartment@interport.net.))
✓ Apartment Store   545-1996
   (Service charge you $145. Listings via fax or e-mail: aptstore@bway.net.)
✓ Homeline   249-9654
   (Service charge: $99 for two month period. Each additional month is $10. Fax only.)

Newspaper Classifieds

Sunday *New York Times* Real Estate section
Village Voice
New York Post
NY Daily News

On Line

- Metro NY Real Estate Guide
http://www.realty.com
for info call 734-9191
- *New York Times* on AOL@ Times
- Real Estate On - Line: http://wwwrealty.com

- *New York Press* Real Estate Search:
http://www.adone.com/nypress/nyp-real.htm
- *Village Voice* Real Estate:
http://www.villagevoice.com/re/

Placing your own wanted posters for living space on various bulletin boards, lampposts, laundromats, universities, and bus stops around town has proven successful for some where newspapers and rental agencies have failed. The posting of flyers in building laundry rooms also seems to work well.

Some flyers even offer rewards for information leading to a vacancy. The flyer should state the type of apartment you are looking for (whether you're looking to share), size, rent, and something about yourself, i.e. responsible, non-smoker, etc. Next, pick your neighborhood that you're interested in and start posting. Some folks around town have landed their own space this way.

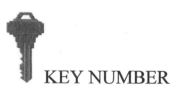

KEY NUMBER

- *Real Estate Complaints*   417-5748
New York State Dept. Of State
Division Of Licensing

IF WORSE COMES TO WORSE CONSIDER A SHARE

Roommate Finders
250 West 57th Street
Suite 1629
New York, NY 10019
489-6862
($200 fee)

The Roommate Solution
488 Madison Avenue
Suite 1700
New York, NY 10022
717-0144
($195 fee)

#39

THE CONCRETE JUNGLE

A compendium of empowerment strategies, rat race tips, hard facts, and consumer advice for fighting back against the New York blues.

If you find yourself in an elevator that's snapped it's cable and is falling fast -- keep jumping up and down in the elevator car.   That way you'll have a 50/50 per cent of surviving the fall.

Car Repair Fraud Bill - The Department of Motor Vehicles now has the authority to shut down any unregistered auto repair shop in New York State.   Under this new law the

DMV will have the power to not only padlock any crooked mechanic - but to remove the shop's machinery just to make sure that he doesn't re-open.

If you're planning a trip with your pet be warned that England, Australia and Hawaii require rather lengthy quarantines. When traveling to Europe you must have a health certificate obtainable from your veterinarian.

HIDDEN ATM CHARGES...Consumers make an average 5 stops per month at them. But using ATM services these days can prove to be costly. Banks usually charge their customers fees when they use an ATM of a different bank. Electronic payment networks such as Cirrus, Nyce and Mac can charge anywhere from fifty cents to two dollars per transaction.

A survey by *Crain's NY Business* found that some hotels and airports use non-traditional ATMs which are not regulated at all and charge higher rates. All in all you're better off using your own bank for ATM services. Don't make more trips than you have to. If your bank doesn't have enough ATMs, consider switching to one that does.

Get A Grip: When traveling use traveler's checks instead of ATMs on unfamiliar ground. A banking account linked to an ATM falls under the jurisdiction of the Electronic Funds Transfer Act which does limit your liability. If you do notice any unauthorized bank transfers on your monthly statement you have to up to 60 days to report it.

39. **SALAD BAR RIP-OFFS**...The Department of Consumer Affairs in the spring of 1996 investigated 37 NYC salad bars and found half of them ripping off customers. The scam is costing New Yorkers an average of 35 cents extra per purchase, sometimes more. Seems some merchants are

fiddling with their scales and failing to deduct the weight of the containers, otherwise known as "tare weight." One store taped six nickels to the bottom of the scale adding one-tenth to the pound. The average salad bar charges $4.99 per pound.

If the scale of the store that you shop in doesn't have a minus feature *before* you place your goodies down, chances are you're overpaying. Speak up and let them know about it.

When shopping at the supermarket, look high and low, not just at eye level where most expensive items tend to be. Make a shopping list and stick to it. Two thirds of all purchases at the supermarket are impulse purchases.

40. **IMPORTANT MOVING ADVICE:** Before you choose a mover, be sure and call the Better Business Bureau to find out how many complaints have been filed against the company. The BBB will give out a rating of either "Satisfactory" or "Unsatisfactory."

Make sure the moving company is fully licensed by calling the Department of Transportation at 718-482-4815. Get an estimate of what the job will cost so there won't be any last minute surprises on your bill.

It's also a good idea to look over your possessions once they are moved into your new residence before signing a delivery receipt. If you have items that are expensive and can't be replaced, get full replacement insurance. You'll feel better and rest a little easier.

In one year alone, over 1,200 complaints were filed against moving & storage companies according to the DCA, BBB, and the State Department of Transportation. Many were unlicensed and advertised at false addresses. For a free brochure (Consumer Guide to Moving & Storage) send a

Storage) send a S.A.S.E to Consumer Affairs Moving & Storage Guide, DCA, 42 Broadway, New York, NY 10004.

41. SOFT SERVE -- A survey conducted in July of 1996 by an independent lab found that 10 out of 11 NYC establishments serving either soft yogurt or ice cream failed to pass health standards.

The study went on to say that high amounts of bacteria were found in the soft serve, caused by employees who either didn't wash their hands or the machinery carefully.

As a precaution, make sure your soft serve is not drip contaminated. If there is any soft serve left on the machine's nozzle going into your cup -- chances are it's loaded with bacteria from the exposure to the air.

Get A Grip: Go to a store that has high volume. That way the product has less chance of standing and accumulating germs.

DINING OUT BLUES...If you're *not* enjoying your meal in a restaurant or find something in it that shouldn't be, don't be reluctant to call over the manager. Very often they'll be happy to offer you a complimentary lunch or dinner just for complaining. Belly-achers not included.

Incidentally, a recent survey was conducted on pet gripes of customers at restaurants -- food was not among them. Lousy service, unfilled water glasses, clearing the table too soon, and hot air hand dryers were more important.

MOST CROWDED SIDEWALK IN LOWER MANHATTAN...The City's planning and transportation department determined that the most crowded sidewalk in Lower Manhattan is Liberty Street just west of Church Street. According to recent findings, 9,146 people cram onto this street on any given morning.

ESCAPE FROM NEW YORK...Allied Van Lines reports one in five people leave New York because it's just too damn crowded. More New Yorkers are moving away from New York State than any other state in the nation. In 1995, 17,000 people left for destinations such as Oregon, North Carolina, Nevada, Florida, and Alaska.

HAVE I STAYED TOO LONG AT THE STREET FAIR? Are street fairs in New York really all they're cracked up to be? As any astute New Yorker will tell you, you're not always getting the best value for your money. I guess some souls believe that paying more for an item means it's superior. Where else can you find New Yorkers shoulder to shoulder willing to fork over a whole dollar for a pickle on a stick? Or those hearty souls who can't wait to lay down 3 bucks for a small order of fries? One of the biggest rip-offs was a booth asking two dollars just for one ear of corn.

Two criticisms against the fairs is that they seem to clone one another and pop up so often (weekly during the spring and summer months). Seems the Mayor's office tends to agree and wants to cut down on a good many of them.

PANIC ATTACK...When running late and stuck in traffic, don't keep looking at your watch. It will do you no good but increase your anxiety level. Biting your lip, swearing or making yourself miserable does nothing to improve the situation. If you feel you're doing the best you can and not getting anywhere, have an alternative plan ready. Get to recognize situations that are beyond your control and don't take it out on yourself.

HARMFUL FOR HUMAN CONSUMPTION...

Shellfish are particularly susceptible to sewage contaminated waters. Eating tainted clams and oysters from poachers who harvest at night is asking for trouble. You leave yourself wide open to food poisoning, hepatitis, and even typhoid. On a local level it is illegal to go shell fishing in Jamaica Bay. More importantly, don't even *think* of eating whatever comes out of it.

FISH POISONING: CITUATERA...

You can't taste it, you can't smell it, you can't cook it out and even more frightening -- most doctors won't recognize it. Dr. Donna Blythe, who specializes in treating Cituatera warns that people eating tropical reef fish such as grouper, red snapper, jack family fish and especially barracuda are most susceptible.

Large predator fish such as the barracuda eat toxic fish who in turn eat the poison from coral reefs. It is then absorbed into their flesh. Vacationing tourists are particularly at risk.

Get A Grip: Eat small fish.

CALL FIRST...

If possible, consider phoning a retail business instead of paying an in-person visit. Many times, phone calls are given priority. If you've had the experience of standing and waiting on line until you're ready to go ballistic you're not alone. This is the clerk's way of telling you he'd rather deal with you anonymously than in your face. Often you can save a good deal of time if you call first.

MOST POLLUTED STREET IN THE CITY --
Madison Avenue. It's no wonder, with scores of buses
utilizing this route fenced in by towering skyscrapers on
either side. Most of us can vouch for how difficult it is to
find the bus stop for the right bus.

Buses are constantly running up this street dumping out
diesel soot, carbon monoxide and other toxins into the air
we breathe. Additionally, taxis, passenger cars, private
and other city bus lines (Triborough, Liberty, Coach, etc.)
make this one street in the city the most polluted.

One of the best ways to spot people from out of town is
to watch for some poor, misguided jogger tearing ass up
Madison Avenue breaking a sweat. Breathe deep. If this
roadway doesn't take the wind out of your sails, nothing
will.

Other parts of the city where pollution prevails include
Fresh Kills Landfill, Pelham Bay Landfill, JFK
International Airport, Greenpoint-Willamsburg, North
River Sewage Treatment Plant, The Gowanus Canal, and
the Lead Belt which is made up of Bedford-Stuyvesant,
Brownsville, Bushwick, and Fort Green owing to their
high levels of lead poisoning.

WORST TIME TO EXERCISE...According to Dr.
Pavlo Toniolo of the Department of Environmental
Medicine at N.Y.U. School of Medicine it is outdoors at
midday in our fair city. The ozone is higher as the sun
warms over high exhaust levels from an overflow of
traffic. Ozone, it has been discovered, can irritate the
respiratory lining and cause bronchitis. "Exercising at
midday may be one of the most dangerous things to do,"
Dr. Toniolo said.

POLLUTION...The National Resources Defense Council reports that New York ranks second for having the worst fine-particle polluted air in the country. The air from Los Angeles came in first causing 5,873 deaths while New York racked up 4,024.

Worst Street In New York...Queens Blvd. Specifically between 62nd drive and 72nd drive in Rego Park. A record 23 people lost their lives in traffic accidents during 1993 on this street.

Worst Bridge in The Nation...According to the Federal Highway Administration, it's New York's very own Triborough Bridge -- in dire need of repair. Coming in second out of the country's 10 worst is our very own Bronx-Whitestone, followed by the Manhattan, Williamsburg, and Macombs Dam bridges.

OUTDOOR CAFES...can only legally operate until midnight on weekdays, and no longer than 1 a.m. on weekends by Department of Consumer Affair guidelines.

NO DEPOSIT, NO RETURN...A five month undercover operation conducted by CBS News discovered that many New Yorkers are being victimized by paying deposit fees on cans and bottles that *cannot* be redeemed. Remember, especially when you're buying beverages by the case, that the container must have a deposit marking on it before it can be redeemed.

DISCRIMINATION IS ALIVE AND WELL...The Human Rights Commission reports that they have no jurisdiction over certain forms of discrimination in New York and elsewhere. Evidently it's still okay to discriminate at private schools *(same sex only classes)*, places of employment (where the staff is less than 4) and private clubs *(ladies drink free)*. On the other hand, it is illegal to be discriminated against for employment, housing and public accommodations on the basis of race, creed, national origin, religious belief, marital status, sexual orientation, disability, citizenship status, or family status. If you suspect you have been, file a complaint with the Commission on Human Rights, 40 Rector Street, NYC, 10006, 212-306-7500.

42. DUCK AND COVER ... When waiting for a pay phone that's in use, *"Don't let the caller see you,"* says psychologist, Steve Feinstein Ph.D. Surveys indicate that in a good many cases, the person on the phone will purposely stay on longer if they see you waiting. It's a territorial non-verbal message about turf protection. Stay out of their sight or carry a cellular phone.

43. MY CABLE IS OUT AGAIN! If you have a problem with your cable company that hasn't been resolved and you want satisfaction -- consider going over their heads by contacting the New York Department of Information, Technology and Telecommunications, 11 Metrotech Center, Brooklyn, NY 11201. (718) 403-1200. You may also get in touch with the NYS Cable Commission, 1-800-342-3330.

WARNING!....Descramblers (cable converters) enable your present cable box to receive all premium channels. They are illegal to purchase in New York State, but there are out-of-state companies (especially in Florida) that sell them openly. Prices vary anywhere between $100-$300, depending on what cable system you have. The cable companies periodically shoot "bullets" (electrical charges) through the system to knock out illegal boxes.

If you're caught with one and haven't notified your cable company, you risk prosecution (for "pirating") and quite possibly paying a $20,000 fine and/or imprisonment. It's been noted that when you bring in your cable box for repairs, your chances of being reported are greater. On the other hand if want to turn anybody in -- call the Cable Theft Hotline 718-670-6511.

44. GETTING YOUR CREDIT REPORT FOR FREE...There are three national credit bureaus: Equifax, TRW, and TransUnion. All three will give you a copy of your credit report. Two will charge you, one will not. It is recommended that you check your credit report for accuracy before making a major purchase, i.e. car, house, or seeking a job that requires a security check.

The one bureau of three that provides you with a complimentary copy once a year is TRW. To obtain a copy you must put your request in writing. Included must be name, address, social security number, date of birth, and proof of residence, i.e. utility bill, driver's license. Send to: TRW Credit Information, Consumer Assistance, PO Box 2350, Chatsworth, CA 91313-2350. Tel., 1-800-392-1122.

TRW   1-800-392-1122 (No charge for report)
Equifax   1-800-685-1111 ($8.00 for report)
TransUnion   1-800-916-8800 ($8.00 for report)

If you've notified the credit bureau of errors in your report and they haven't made corrections, call the Federal Trade Commission at 264-1207.

Organizations that can help you pay it off:

Nat'l Foundation for Consumer Credit   800-388-2227
Budget & Counseling Services   675-5070
Consumer Credit Counseling Service   800-388-2223
Shopaholics Limited   675-4345

Get A Grip: Negotiating a lower interest rate with your credit card company is better than not paying off your debt.

45. **GRABBING A PEEK AT YOUR SECRET MEDICAL RECORDS**...Chances are your medical report is available to everybody and their brother just for the asking. To find out if yours is accurate, why not request a copy to see what's being said about you? You will first need to fill out a short form by calling the Medical Information Bureau at 617-426-3660. Or you may write to the bureau itself at: MIB, PO Box 105, Essex Station, Boston, MA 02112. (If you dispute any of the information in the report, write a letter to MIB with the following: list the item, the report number, the reporting company, and the date of the report.)

46. **DRY CLEANING CATASTROPHES**...Suppose your local dry cleaner has lost your favorite blouse or put a new stain on Uncle Harry's suit where there was none before? Take aim. First, it's to your benefit to try to work it out with the merchant and reach an amicable agreement, if for no other reason than saving you time.

If a reasonable solution is not in your immediate future, file a complaint with the Department of Consumer Affairs, 487-4398. Concurrently, contact the NCA

(Neighborhood Cleaners Association) at 252 West 29th Street, New York, NY 10001. Phone 212-967-3002.

The NCA is a 50-year-old voluntary trade association that has over 1200 professional dry cleaners and 90% membership in Manhattan.

The NCA will try to negotiate a fair settlement between merchant and customer. On the other hand, if you still find the agreement or lack of one unacceptable, your next step may be Small Claims Court.

Get-A- Grip: No certification or training is required in order to open up a dry cleaning establishment.

DANGER...If you live above a dry cleaning establishment you might be exposed to harmful levels of a poisonous dry cleaning fluid. The central nervous system is affected by the toxic chemical Perchloroethylene (Perc) which is linked to nausea, headaches, liver, kidney damage, and cancer. New York State law prohibits dry cleaners in residential buildings, New York City laws do not. Contact: Dept. of Environmental Conservation on this one (718-482-4944) as well as the Department of Health's Environmental Investigations unit at 442-9666.

Get A Grip: Don't forget to take your clothes out of the plastic that comes with your dry cleaned goods as soon as you get home. Don't just hang the bag in the closet and forget about it. The fumes contained in the garment need to be aired out.

47. **JURY DUTY**....Effective January 1, 1996 in New York State -- there are no more occupational exemptions. Anyone and everyone must now report for jury selection. Only if you can prove extreme hardship or if your business is in Chapter 11 (be prepared to bring in personal and corporate returns as proof) will you be excused.

Compensation was at $15.00 per day plus transportation. However, it is expected to rise to $27.50 per day as of February 1, 1997 and then to skyrocket to a whopping $40 per day beginning February 1, 1998.

Most New Yorkers feel that having to go through Jury Duty is a frustrating waste of time. But now due to court reform, judges will oversee the jury process in civil cases instead of leaving it up to lawyers who have been known to keep jurors waiting endlessly and to subject them to never-ending questioning.

Incidentally, if you are fined for not responding to your juror summons and it goes unpaid, it goes on your record. If you find yourself requesting a mortgage or a line of credit -- it's there for the world to see.

48. **RED LIGHT RUNNING**...The Red Light Camera Program is a new way of tracking vehicles whose owners break the law. The program enables cameras, at various   locations, to take photos of license plates as well as verify the speed of lawbreakers. The photo is used to issue a ticket automatically to the driver. To date more than 370,000 tickets have been issued to motorists in NYC since its inception in December 1993.

Currently there are about 27 Red Light spy cameras positioned   throughout the city, according to the

Department of Transportation. If you're caught, it's a $50 fine.

Manhattan Red Light Camera Locations:
Houston and West Sts southbound
42nd St and 7th Ave southbound
72nd St and 3rd Ave northbound
72nd St and Amsterdam Ave northbound

Bronx Locations:
149th St. and 3rd Ave. Southbound
161st St. and Anderson Ave. Eastbound
Major Deegan Service Rd & Yankee Stadium northbound
Cross Bronx Expy Service Rd & Rosedale Ave westbound
Pelham Pkwy and Stillwell Ave westbound
Grand Concourse and E. 167th St (north & southbound)

Queens Locations:
Queens Blvd and 58th St all directions
Queens Blvd and Ascam Ave all directions
Northern Blvd and Douglaston Parkway westbound
Rockaway Parkway and Brookville Rd. westbound
South Conduit Ave and 89th St eastbound

Brooklyn Locations:
Pennsylvania Ave and Atlantic Ave eastbound
Ocean Parkway and Church Ave northbound
Bay Parkway and 65th St northbound
Hamilton Avenue and Clinton St northbound
Hamilton Ave and 60th St westbound
Fort Hamilton Parkway and 60th St westbound
Boerum Place and Atlantic Ave southbound
Coney Island Ave and Avenue J northbound
Flatbush Ave before Toys R Us store southbound
4th Ave and 41st St southbound

Staten Island
Hylam Blvd and Burbank Ave northbound
Victory Blvd and Morani Ave eastbound

For additional information on red light camera locations, visit the web site; *http://www.panix.com:80/~sshah/ss-nyred.htm*

49. SAVE $$$ RENTING A CAR...It may be cheaper for you to walk in off the street instead of calling and making a reservation, according to a survey of car rental establishments. If the company sees that cars in the lot are not moving, they're more apt to give you a better deal. By the way, if you didn't know it yet, New York has the most expensive rates in the whole country.

Reasonably priced car rental outlets:

Village Rent-a-Car 19 E. 12th St.	243-9200
National Car Rental	800-227-7368

Incidentally, are you, like most of us, confused about what kind of car insurance to purchase when renting? Your credit card may cover this expense. It is advisable to check first with your credit card company. If you have any other questions, call the *National Insurance Consumer Helpline* 800-942-4242.

50. PULLING THE PLUG ON JUNK MAIL... You come home from a hard day only to find your mailbox stuffed like a cabbage. If only you could just get your issue of *Popular Mechanics* out of the mailbox in one piece. An average family gets 100 pounds of junk mail every year, not to mention the acres of forests that we lose in the process.

Solicitations from charities, letters telling you've won five nights and four days in the Poconos, as well as an entire deluge of recycled offers. Enough is enough.

Want your name removed from present and future mailing lists?

Write to: *Direct Marketing Association's Mail Preference Service*, PO Box 9008, Farmingdale, NY 11735 or call the Mail & Telephone Preference Service, 202-955-5030. You may also contact *Private Citizen*, an organization dedicated to protect privacy rights (800-CUT-JUNK).

Bob Bulmash, president of Private Citizen, recommends calling the firm sending you junk mail. Tell them to stop. They in turn will tell you that they will -- but in all likelihood they probably won't completely.

Get-A-Grip : Instruct them that you are about to change your address and give them your congressman's address instead. Let your legislator get a sample of junk mail first hand. Some practices need to be experienced by those representing you in local government. Then and only then we can hope for legislation curtailing this obnoxious practice.

Stopping junk e-mail on your computer: Call 1-888-970-JUNK (Zero Junk Mail service charges about $15 a year). Or visit their web site at www.zerojunk.com

51. **WHERE'S THERE'S SMOKE**...there's usually some inconsiderate, self-centered jerk with a cigarette. Cigarette smoke contains more than 4,000 chemicals including 40 that have been know to cause cancer. Among them: carbon monoxide, carbon dioxide, nicotine, methane, formaldehyde, and cyanide. No smoking is allowed in a restaurant that has 35 or more seats in the dining area according to the Smoke Free Air

Act, Local Law #5. The Board of Health's non-smoking enforcement unit will hand out summonses to any offending establishment. Just be persistent and don't forget to follow up.

Notify the NY Board of Health, 280 Broadway, Room 301, NYC, 10007 (442-1838). Any eatery having less than 35 seats remains exempt from the law. Legislation was originally defeated aimed at banning smoking in *all* public places, but a watered down version (The Smoke-Free Air Act) is now the law. Current research indicates that non-smokers are more vulnerable to heart damage from secondhand smoke because they haven't built up the defenses against tobacco poison that smokers have.

The Department of Health estimates that each year 3,000 American nonsmokers die from lung cancer caused by secondhand smoke. *A study by Cornell University revealed that 74% of us these days are non-smokers.*

The Most Dangerous Intersection...According to Borough President Ruth Messinger's office, 14,000 pedestrians are either injured or killed on New York City streets each year due to motorists failing to drive cautiously and obey safety rules.

The most dangerous intersection in the city remains a first place tie between 33rd Street and Park Avenue South and West 42nd Street and Eighth Avenue. Both crossings had 65 accidents involving pedestrians from January 1989 through August 1994.

Worst Intersections For Pedestrians

☠ 33rd St & Broadway   (43 accidents)
☠ Bruckner Blvd at Hunts Point Ave(37 accidents)
☠ Eastern Pkwy at Utica Ave   (36 accidents)
☠ 34th Street & 8th Ave   (35 accidents)
☠ 125th Street and Lenox Ave   (29 accidents)
☠ Jamaica Ave at Pasons Blvd   (28 accidents)
☠ Hillside Ave at Parsons Blvd   (27 accidents)

The Most Accident-Prone Roadway ...in the State of New York is the interchange between the Cross Bronx and Bruckner expressways, says the State Transportation Department. Between 1992 and 1994, 171 accidents occurred on this roadway.

How To Beat The Toll To Long Island & Queens...Why pay a toll on The Triborough Bridge or the Queens Midtown Tunnel when you can get there for free? From Manhattan: take the Queensboro Bridge on 59th Street. Stay right, then get on route 25 to Van Dam Street. Go right on Van Dam Street. Continue down to the next overramp. Turn right and go straight out to route 495, the Long Island Expressway.

Get a Grip: Van Dam Street is the last exit before tolls. Don't get off at exit 16. Wait until Van Dam Street.

Most Dangerous Profession...Is by far being a New York City cab driver, according to The National Institute for Occupational Safety and Health. Cabbies have a greater chance of being murdered on the job than any other profession.

Not Quite The Worst Airport...JFK Airport was rated 40th out of 43 airports worldwide for convenience, comfort, and customer service in a survey by the International Air Transport Association. Among those rated lower than the US were Tokyo, Athens, and Paris. Manchester Airport in England was rated number one.

New York City ranked 23rd in crime out of the nation's 25 largest cities in 1996. Only San Diego and San Jose had lower crime rates. Rated the most dangerous were Baltimore, Washington, D.C., and Detroit.

52. **GETTING THE LEAD OUT**... I don't know about you, but somehow knowing that there's lead poison lurking in my drinking water is enough to put a damper on lunch at Waterside Plaza.

Lead accumulates in the blood, bones, and soft tissues of the body as well as in the nervous system. Excessive exposure can lead to seizures and behavior disorders. Particularly vulnerable are children. The best advice may not be running out and buying the most expensive water filter.

The Department of Environmental Protection recommends leaving the cold tap on because it is less corrosive than warm and contains less lead. Run it about a minute in your home if it hasn't been used in more than six hours. This will help flush out water that has been contaminated by lead in the pipes. You can request the DEP's guidelines on lead levels by calling (718) DEP-HELP.

CRYPTOSPORIDIOSIS...an illness caused by a single-celled parasite has been found in the New York drinking water supply. By ingesting this bug, symptoms such as diarrhea, vomiting, fever, and headache can arise. Some preventive measures are washing your hands before handling food, after using the toilet, handling animals, or gardening.

Boiling all tap water for at least one minute is also advisable. According to recent findings from the Health Department, we're all susceptible to this infection. Further information can be obtained from the DEP at 718-595-6600 and the Health Department at 212-442-1999.

53. **HOW NOT TO GET TICKETED AT A BROKEN PARKING METER**... Presently there are 67,000 parking meters in New York City so it's only natural that one or two might be on the fritz. Parking meters in NYC have been around since September 19, 1951. When they do break down these days, you can forget about putting a brown bag over one. According to traffic enforcement officers, it rarely works. (To complain about defective parking meters, call NYC Traffic Dept. 718-830-7500). You've got a far better chance by having a neat little traffic aide known as *Parking Pal* on your side.

Parking Pal is a bright green laminated sheet (to be placed in your car window) identifying your right as a motorist to park at a broken meter. Technically you may park for the maximum time permitted at the meter and where there is no legible parking sign posted. This motorist's aid was developed by New York legal researcher Louis Camporeale, who spent hours examining city traffic laws in an effort to shed new light on motorist's rights.

Parking Pal lets traffic enforcement officers know that you're aware of your legal rights under NYC traffic law. In the event of a wrongful ticket, the kit comes complete with instructions on getting the DOT to dismiss the summons. It sells for just $6.95 plus $1.00 shipping. *Parking Pal* also offers Commercial and Medical Profession editions of the product for $8.95 plus $1.00 shipping. For more information, write to: *Parking Pal, PO Box 350-003, Dept. GG, Bklyn, NY 11235.*

FYI...The city plans to remove about 4,000 fire hydrants in lower Manhattan that have not been active for ages. It's been reported that this move will make way for 4,850 new parking spaces. The bad news...? More parking meters.

You can save a fortune when planning to buy your next automobile by attending one of the PVB's car auctions. The auctions are held throughout the five boroughs at independent garages and by the NYC Sheriff's office.

54. **EMS COMPLAINTS**...Emergency medical service personnel often can mean the difference between life and death. New York City residents have reason to worry. The average wait time of an ambulance for cardiac arrest is almost 9 minutes. That's one of the slowest responses in the country.

If you have a complaint with either an EMS, private or a voluntary hospital ambulance (and assuming you're still around to voice it) put it all in writing. Send it to: NYS Dept. of Health, EMS Program, 5 Penn Plaza, 5th floor, Complaint Dept., NYC 10001.

Because there are only three investigators working for the entire five boroughs, allow about eight weeks for a follow up.

Get A Grip: In 1995 there were 10.1 million calls made to 911 in New York City.

55. **LOUSY COPS**...You filed a complaint with your local precinct and they didn't take your complaint seriously. Perhaps it was the desk sergeant who blew you off or quite possibly a local patrol car (assuming you can find one) failed to respond. In 1995, about 5,689 complaints were filed with the Civilian Complaint Review Board (CCRB).

An increase of 135% from the prior year. 2,232 of those complaints were for rude behavior alone. The CCRB (800-341-CCRB) is an independent agency which has the authority to investigate charges and make recommendations to the Police Commissioner.

Complaints fall into four categories: excessive or unnecessary force, abuse of authority, discourtesy, and offensive language. Besides filing a complaint with the CCRB, sending a duplicate letter to the commander of the precinct as well as to the Police Commissioner is recommended for making sure that your message is heard.

It should be understood that the CCRB does not have the authority to discipline police officers. That final determination rests with the Police Commissioner. What's not encouraging is that very few cops ever receive stiff penalties. In 1995, no police officer was suspended or terminated as a result of a CCRB complaint. In roughly about 5% of the cases, the CCRB was able to authenticate the complaint and advocated disciplinary action. Seems those complaining don't always follow through or don't show up for hearings.

The sad reality is that the heaviest punishment ever handed out is in the form of lost vacation days. Still, it is advisable to complain when you feel you've been wronged. Even if the police officer in question does not get suspended, it is a mark against his or her record when it comes time for a promotion.

Some believe that the CCRB is basically an ineffectual agency, and civil liberties attorneys believe a more effective solution to severe charges is suing the city. In the fiscal year of 1995, New York City paid out a record $300 million in court awards.

12 NEW YORK EATERIES
#40   OPEN ALL NIGHT

It's tough when you've got a case of the late night munchies and no restaurant is within striking distance.

Listed are 12 of the eateries that remain open through the wee hours of the morning.

Empire Diner
210 Tenth Av (22nd St.)
243-2736

Market Diner
572 Eleventh Av (43 St.)
695-0415

The Brasserie
100 East 53rd St.
751-4840

Around the Clock Cafe
8 Stuyvesant Place
598-0402

Tramway Coffee Shop
1143 Second Av (60th)
758-7017

Veselka
144 Second Av (9th St.)
228-9682

Viand
300 East 86th St. (2nd Av)
879-9425

Omega
122 West 72nd St.
874-2000 (Fri-Sat)

Green Kitchen
1477 First Ave (77th St.)
988-4163

French Roast
458 Sixth Ave (11th St.)
533-2233

Hong Fat
63 Mott St (Canal St)
962-9588

Kiev International
117 Second Av (6th St.)
674-4040

7 THINGS TO DO IN NEW YORK WHEN YOU AIN'T GOT ANY MONEY

1.   Take a ride in one of the glass elevators at the *Marriott Marquis Hotel* (45th Street and Broadway) and feel your stomach drop. It's almost as good as going to Coney Island.

2.   Go to *Downstairs Records* (35 West 43rd Street) and play some great rock and roll records on their turntable.

3.   Visit a shop called *Aphrodisia* in the Greenwich Village (264 Bleecker Street) and try some different aromatherapy scents.   Smell a rainbow and play with the 3 cats who live there.

4.   Check out the newly-opened *Borders* book store at 5 World Trade Center. Open a book or magazine. Listen to a free lecture.

5.   Go sit on a bench in the dog run at Washington Square Park near NYU.   Shmooze or throw a tennis ball to one of the pooches and watch them dance for you.

6.   Visit the trade show of your choice at the *Javits Convention Center* (11th Avenue and 35th Street). The way to get in without paying is to show them your business card if it relates to the industry. Otherwise keep some all-purpose generic cards to fit the ocassion. *(Hint: if one clerk does not admit you - walk down a ways and try another.)*

7.   Check out *The Sharper Image* (locations throughout the city) and get a free massage on one of their vibrating chairs.

"I have all I can stands and I can't stands no more!"

Popeye

#42

AN ARSENAL OF KEY CONTACTS NO NEW YORKER SHOULD <u>EVER</u> BE WITHOUT

EMERGENCIES

Doctors on call	238-2100
Crime Victims Line	577-7777
Police-Fire-Ambulance	911
(* for more medical information see	
Hospital Emergency Rooms chapter)	

Con Edison gas emergency	683-8830
Electric or steam emergency	683-0862
	338-3000

Missing Credit Cards

Amex	800-528-4800
MasterCard	800-627-8372
Visa	800-336-8472

LATE NIGHT PHARMACIES

<u>Open 24 hours</u>

Duane Reade	57th St & B'way	541-9708
Kaufman Pharmacy	557 Lexington Av (50 St.)	755-2266
Genovese Drug Store	13-19 E. 8th St	982-7325
Buckingham Chemists	1405 Sixth Ave (57 St.)	247-2014

till midnight* (*except Sunday - until 9 PM)

Complaints on Pharmicists: NYS Department of Education,
Board of Pharmacy   951-6400

TRANSIT INFORMATION

Subway & Bus Information	718-330-1234
NYC Transit Lost & Found	718-625-6200
Amtrack	800-872-7245
Carey's Airport Buses	718-632-0509
Express Bus Service (outer boroughs)	994-5500
Air Ride Buses	800-247-7433
Geo. Washington Bridge Bus Station	564-1114
Greyhound Buses	971-6363
Hoboken-Battery Ferry	201-420-6307
Long Island RR	718-217-LIRR
Metro North	532-4900
Metro North Lost & Found	340-2555
Metroliner	800-523-8720
Path Trains (Hudson Tubes)	800-234-7284
Lost & Found	435-2611
NJ Transit (in NJ)	800-772-2222
NJ Transit (out of state)	201-762-5100
Port Authority	564-8484
Port Imperial Ferry	800-53-FERRY
New York Road Conditions	566-3406
Shadow Traffic Report	566-4121
Staten Island Ferry	806-6940
Staten Island Rapid Transit	718-447-8601
Statue of Liberty Ferry	718-390-5253
Downtown Manhattan Heliport	248-7240
New York Helicopter	800-645-3494
34th Street Heliport	889-0986
West 30th St Heliport	563-4442

AIRPORTS

LaGuardia	718-533-3400
LaGuardia Lost & Found	718-533-3988
JFK International	718-244-4444
JFK Lost & Found	718-244-4225
Newark	201-961-6000
Newark Lost & Found	201-961-6230

VISITOR INFORMATION

NY Visitors Bureau	2 Columbus Circle	397-8222
Arts & Festival Information		765-ARTS
Traveler's Aid Society	160 West 42nd St	944-0013
Radio City Music Hall	50th St & 6th Ave	247-4777
Carneige Hall	57th St & 7th Ave	247-7800
City Center	131 West 55th St	581-1212
Metropolitan Opera	Lincoln Center (66 St)	362-6000
Avery Fisher Hall	Lincoln Center (66 St)	875-5030
Shea Stadium	126th St & Roosevelt Ave	718-507-8499
Yankee Stadium	161st St & River Ave	718-293-6000

GOING TO THE THEATER CHEAP

Audience Extras - 109 West 26th St	989-9550
Theater Development Fund - 1501 B'way	221-0885
Hit Show Club - 630 9th Ave	581-4211

COMPLAINTS & GENERAL INFO

AA meeting (nearest meeting)	647-1680
Animals - Humane Treatment	876-7700
City Council Information Desk	788-7101
City Council Hotline	788-7127
District Attorney, Manhattan	335-9000
FBI	384-1000
Green Card Information	718-899-4000

Heat, Hot Water, Mantinence (Dept. Of Housing)	960-4800
Nearest AA meeting	647-1680
Mayor's Action Line(complaints)	788-7594
Mail: Fraud, Theft, Obscene	330-3305
Monuments, Info	935-3960
Passport & Visa Info, (630 Fifth Ave)	399-5290
Pothole complaints	POT-HOLE
Public Library Info-Locations	340-0849
US Secret Service	466-4400
Sidewalk Repairs	323-8501
Sleep Hotline	434-2000
Suicide Prevention Line	673-3000
Telephone Crisis Line	532-2400
Treatment/Prevention of head lice	800-446-4NPA
Parking Violations Help Line	477-4430
Parks Department Complaints	800-834-3832
Pet transportation (Pet Cab)	491-5300
US Customs, JFK Airport	718-553-1824
Unemployment Insurance (Tel Service)	718-488-1800
Western Union: Telegrams	800-325-6000
Zip Code Information	967-8585

TAKING ACTION NUMBERS

Advocate for the Disabled	800-522-4369
AIDS Hotline	807-6655
NYS AIDS Hotline	800-872-2777
Alcoholics Anonymous	647-1680
NYS Alcohol & Substance Abuse	800-522-5353
Bias Hotline	662-2427
Blind/Visually Handicapped Library	800-342-3688
NYS Breast Cancer Hotline	800-877-8077
Bureau of Day Camps and Recreation	643-4311
Cancer Information Service	800-4-CANCER
NYS Child Abuse Crisis Line	800-342-3720
City Agencies (touch tone)	788-4636
State Agencies	488-4141
Federal Agencies	800-347-1997

City Board of Elections	886-3800
City Council Meetings	788-7127
Coast Guard	668-7936
Cocaine Anonymous	496-4266
Cocaine Hotline	800-262-2463
Day Care Complaint Hotline	800-732-5207
Domestic Violence Crisis Line	800-942-6906
Senior Citizens Info & Referral	800-342-9871
Gay and Lesbian Switchboard	777-1800
Growing Up Healthy Hotline	800-342-9871
Herpes Hotline	628-9154
Incest Survivors Hotline	227-3000
American Immigration Lawyers	202-371-9377
Mental Health Counseling Hotline	734-5876
Mood Disorders Support Group	533-MDSG
Narcotics Anonymous	718-805-9835
Poison Control Center	340-4494
NY Public Library Phone Reference	340-0849
Rape Hotline	267-7273
Runaways Hotline	619-6884
NYS Senior Citizens Hotline	800-342-9871
Sex Crimes Crisis Lines	267-7273
NYS Dept of Social Services Info	800-342-3009
Status of bills, State Senate	800-342-9860
Tax Help	718-935-6736
Teacher, Dial-A- (homework)- Mon-Thur 4-7pm	777-3380
Travel Agents Accredited	516-747-4716
Wage, Hour div. of Dept. of Labor	264-8185
Westside Rifle-Pistol Range, 20 W 20 St.	243-9448
Youth Hotline	800-246-4646

UH-OH, IT'S ONE OF THOSE DAYS

AUTO PROBLEMS

NY Auto Repair 236 W. 60th Street	307-7940
Lafayette Tire & Auto Lafayette & Houston	925-1516

Parking Ticket Hotline   477-4430
Ticket Fighters   666-6514

BROKEN CAR WINDOWS?

Discount Auto Glass   616 W. 49th St   977-5877
Liberty Glass   546 W. 48th St   265-3052

FEDERAL, STATE, CITY AGENCY CONTACTS

Social Security Office (To check your present earnings
and retirement benefits for accuracy)   800-772-1213

Rent Guidelines Board   349-2262
rent increases and other information

City Dept of Health   442-1999
provides referral numbers for information
and complaints about communicable disease
surveillance, lead poisoning, window guards,
pest control, water quality, problems with
restaurant food or bakery goods, animal bites
and licenses, no smoking ordiances

Dept of Environmental Conservation 718-482-4949
enforces Environmental Conservation Law;
maintains air and water quality; manages
hazardous toxic and solid waste

Dept of Environmental Protection   718-699-9811
manages city water supply and wastewater
system; handles hazardous material emergencies
and asbestos monitoring and removal; enforces
city's noise code; handles complaints about backed-up
sewers and foul odors

**City Dept of Health,
Professional Medical Conduct Division**   613-2650
handles complaints concerning physician misconduct

Better Business Bureau   533-6200
gives consumer advice and information about
charities and companies; files complaints

City Dept of Housing Preservation   960-4800
handles heat and hot water complaints and other
code violations

City Dept of Transportation   442-7070
fixes broken street and traffic lights

Civilian Complaint Review Board   442-8833
investigates and recommends action concerning
police misconduct

Dept of Agriculture and Markets   718-722-2876
receives complaints about supermarket food;
enforces Kosher food laws

Dept of Buildings   312-8530
handles structural complaints for
construction sites

Mayor's Action Center   788-7585
provides infomation, receives complaints and
resolves problems with city services

Dept of Sanitation Action Center   219-8090
collects garbage, dead animals on the streets,
clears snow, cleans vacant lots; removes derelict
vehicles, complaints

Postmaster, New York   330-3668
monitors late or non-delivery of mail

US Postal Inspector   330-3602
investigates mail fraud, obscene mail and
service complaints

New York Dept of State   417-5800
complaints about state agencies

Complaints about HMOs or Health Providers
NYS Insurance Dept.   602-0203

Complaints about Investment Brokers
NYS Investor Protection & Securities
120 Broadway, 23rd Floor
New York, NY 10271
(It is advisable to put your complaint in writing)   416-8222

To check out a broker in advance contact:
National Association of Securities Dealers   800-289-9999

Real Estate Difficulties... Whether it's an unethical
slimeball trying to take unfair advantage or hidden clauses in
the fine print. Questions or complaints are received by the
NYS Dept. Of State, div. of licensing at
                                                      417-5748

Movies and TV Production Complaints... Unsafe
conditions, obstruction of commercial or residential traffic --
The Mayor's office of Film & Broadcasting needs to know

                                                      489-6710

COMMUNITY BOARDS

Community Board # 1 51 Chambers St. 10007
area: the Battery to south of Canal Street - East River to Hudson River
Chairperson: Ann Compoccia   442-5050

Community Board # 2 3 Washington Sq Village 10012
area: Canal St to 14th St - Bowery to Hudson Sts.
Chairperson: Benjamin Green   979-2272

Community Board # 3 59 East 4th St. 10003
area: 14th St to Brooklyn Bridge - East River to Bowery
Chairperson: Albert Fabozzi   533-5300

Community Board # 4 330 West 42nd St 10036
area: N. 14th St. to 26th St (West of 6th Ave) 26th - 59th Sts. (West of 8th ave)
Chairperson: Jo Ann Macy   736-4536

Community Board # 5 450 7th Ave. 10123
area: 14th St. to 59th St - Lexington to 8th Ave
(ex, Chelsea, Murray Hill, Grammercy)
Chairperson: Nicholas Fish   465-0907

Community Board # 6 330 East 26th St. 10010
area: 14th St to 59th St. - East River to Lex - 34th to 40th up to Madison Ave
Chairperson: Gary Papush   679-0907

Community Board # 7 250 West 87th St. 10024
area: 59th St & Central Park West to 110th & Henry Hudson Pkwy
Chairperson: Diane Bratcher   362-4008

Community Board # 8   309 East 94th St. 10128
area: N. 59th St to South 96th St. - 5th Ave to East River
includes Roosevelt Island
Chairperson: Carolyn M. Greenberg   427-4840

Community Board # 9   565 West 125th St. 10027
area: South 110th St to West to River - East to St. Nicholas
Ave.
Chairperson: Marita Dunn   864-6200

Community Board # 10   215 West 125th St. 10027
area: West of 5th Ave & 110th St - W of 8th Ave to 158th
Chairperson: Barbara Askins   749-3105

Community Board # 11   55 East 115th St. 10029
area: N. 96th St - 142 St. East River to East of 5th Ave.
Chairperson: Eddie Baca   831-8929

Community Board # 12   711 West 168th St. 10032
area: W. 155th St to W. 218th St - river to river
Chairperson: Sander Dulitz   568-8500

To locate your Community Board District call the
League of Women Voters Information Service
212-674-8484.

#43

HOW TO TAWK
LIKE A NEW YAWKER

Speaking New Yawkese is more of an attitude. Your mouth begins to have a life all it's own. Here are some key words that are indigeneous to the city that never sleeps but could use a short nap.

Ant-Knee   you remember Ant-knee and Cleopatra?

Awda   "waiter we're ready to awda."

Ax   as in " I would like to ax you a question."

Bagel   a hard and crusty roll, soft inside and shaped like a small life preserver.

Bialy   pronounced "bee-ollie". A slightly underbaked roll with baked onion sprinkled on it.

Cawfee   available in decaf or industrial strength.

Chawklit   who can resist this dessert?

Chutzpah   nerve, gall.

D'Jeet ?   an inquiry as to whether you had lunch or dinner.

Egg Cream   seltzer, chocolate syrup (Fox's U-Bet), a dash of milk stirred in a glass.

Feh   an expression of displeasure "Did you like the movie? Feh!"

Fuckin' A   an exclamation of pleasure, triumph.

Godda   as in must. "I godda go."

Halvah   a candy made with crushed sesame seeds and honey, and sold in neighborhood delis. Originally made in Turkey.

Hassle   anything in New York that detains you for more than 30 seconds.

Howawya   a greeting: as in "Howawya?"

IRT   code name for one such subway line.
                 Complete with subway loudspeaker
                 announcements by those creatures with a
                 degree in gibberish. An interpreter is
                 highly recommended.

Jap   Jewish american princess/prince

Kaput   inoperative, ineffective.

Klutz   a clumsy bumbler, an oaf

Knish   dumplings filled with grated potatoes,
                 onions, chopped liver or cheese, deep
                 fried. The good ones lie in your stomach
                 for a week.

Kvetch   *verb.* to complain loudly over and over (as
                 in hassle).
                 noun. a person who complains repeatedly.

Lemmie   as in "lemmie a quarter will ya?"

Mensch   a good man. A gentleman.

Seltzer   fizzy beverage made by charging water with
                 carbon dioxide.

Schlep   *verb.* to carry a heavy package with difficulty.
                 noun. an unkempt, untidy wet blanket.

Schmear   to spread something massively on something
                 else, i.e. cream cheese on a bagel.

Schmuck   a dope, a jerk, penis
                (gentiles usually pronounce it without the
                c-h sound making it, *Smuck*)

Schmooze   shooting the breeze. Small talk.

Witcha   to go along. "Take me witcha."

Yo   as in "what's yo name?"

Zilch   zero, nothing.

Get a Grip: It's been said that if you can't say anything good
about a person, say it in Yiddish.

#44

23 REASONS <u>NOT</u> TO LEAVE NEW YORK
(at least for January & February...well maybe part of July too)
(I'm not making this stuff either)

1. **Get Out Your Boxer Shorts Day,**
    Jan. 4 - Waco, N.C.

2. **National Pass Gas Day,**
    Jan. 7 - Dallas, TX

3. **Cuckoo Dancing Week,**
    Jan 11-17, Michigan

4. **National Nothing Day,**
    Jan 16, Nevada

5. **Chicago's Freak Gas Explosion Anniversary,**
    Jan. 17, Chicago

6. **Humpback Whale Awareness Month,**
    Jan. 1-28, Walmanalo, Hawaii

7. **Flouride Day,**
    Jan. 25 - Grand Rapids, MI

8. **Thomas Crapper Day** (inventor of the flush toilet)
    Jan. 27 - England

9. **Backwards Day,**
    Jan 28, Indiana

10.   **National Kazoo Day,**
       Jan. 28, Chambersburg, PA

11.   **Gilroy Garlic Festival,**
       Jan. 29-31, Gilroy, CA

12.   **National Prune Breakfast Month,**
       Jan.1-31 -   San Francisco

13.   **The Testicle Festival,**
       Jan (?), Clinton, Montana,
       (couldn't they of picked a warmer month?)

14.   **Return Shopping Carts to the Supermarket Month,**
       February, Chicago

15.   **Frankly, I Don't Give A Damn Day,**
       Feb. 1 - Cadiz, Ohio

16.   **Eva Braun Birthday Anniversary,**
       Feb. 6, Munich, Germany

17.   **Put Your Gun Away Day**
       Feb. 7, Los Angeles

18.   **National Kraut & Weenie Week,**
       Feb 10-19, Edison, New Jersey

19.   **Canned Food Month,**
       Feb 1-28, Chicago

20.   **National Fiber Focus Month,**
       Feb 1-28, Minneapolis

21. **I've Got A Rash I Can't Explain Day,**
Feb. 17 - Oxnard, CA

22. **Spaghetti Bridge Building Contest,**
Feb. 17, Kelowna, BC, Canada

23. **Minnesota Sit and Spit Club Convention**
and Cherry Pit Spitting Contest,
July 23, Mankato, MN

Source: Chase's Annual Events

#45   FINDING YOUR WAY AROUND THE BIG CITY

Getting lost in the big city is part of the fun. But just in case you're looking to find your street address in a hurry here are some quick tips on how to find your destination.

Drop the final digit from the address. Divide the remaining figure in half and add or subtract the number indicated below. Your result will be the number of the nearest cross street.

> ### NEW YORK FUN FACT
>
> For every New Yorker who thinks he is lost -- there are approximately 2.3 New Yorkers who *actually* are.

First Ave		Add	3
Second Ave		Add	3
Third Ave		Add	10
Lexington Ave		Add	22
Fourth Ave		Add	8
Park Ave		Add	35
Madison Ave		Add	26
Fifth Ave	up to 200	Add	13
	up to 400	Add	16
	up to 600	Add	18
	up to 775	Add	20
	775-1286	Sub	18
	cancel last figure		
	up to 1500	Add	45
	above 2000	Add	24
Sixth Ave	Ave of Americas	Sub	12
Seventh Ave		Add	12
	Above 110th	Add	20
Eighth Ave		Add	10

Ninth Ave		Add 13
Tenth Ave		Add 14
Amsterdam Ave		Add 60
Broadway	23-192 Sts.	Sub 30
Columbus Ave		Add 60
Riverside Dr	divide house number by 10 and add 72 up to 165th Street	
West End Ave		Add 60
York Ave		Add 3

KEY NUMBER

- *Transit Authority - Transit Information*   718-330-1234

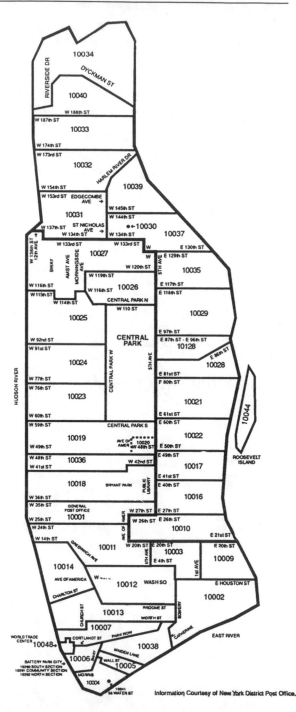

Information Courtesy of New York District Post Office.

INDEX

ORDER AN ADDITIONAL COPY OF

GET-A-GRIP NEW YORK - BOOK II

AND RECEIVE A COPY OF THE
GET-A-GRIP NEWSLETTER
COMPLETE WITH ALL RECENT UPDATES *FREE* !

send check or money order to:

StreetBeat Publications
P.O. Box 32 - Ansonia Station
New York, NY 10023-0032

Number of copies @ $12.95 each   _____

Shipping & Handling   _____
($1.75 for the first book, $.75 for each additional book)

TOTAL   _____

(Please Print)

Name _____

Address_____Apt.____

City/State/Zip_____

HEY NEW YORK...
GET A GRIP
ON THE *NOISE!*

CITIQUIET ™

Interior Noise Elimination Windows

. No Building Approval . No Construction Necessary .
. Totally Operable . Completely Removable .
. Custom Manufactured to Compliment Any Window Style .
. ELIMINATES 100% DRAFT and DIRT .
. Also, Noise Elimination Walls, Ceilings and Floors .

NOISE ELIMINATION AT 100%SATISFACTION.

212-8-SILENCE
888-4-SILENCE

218 EAST 81st STREET NEW YORK, N.Y. 10028

Tackle heartburn with something your body needs anyway.

Tums has calcium. Many antacids don't. Maalox and Mylanta Liquids and Tablets use
aluminum and magnesium. Tums helps wipe out heartburn and gives you calcium you need every day.
©1995 SmithKline Beecham Consumer Healthcare. Use only as directed.

ABOUT THE AUTHOR

Raymond Alvin is a graduate of the School of Hard Knocks. A born and bred New Yorker, he is the editor of the *GET-A-GRIP NEWSLETTER* which focuses on tips, strategies and the art of survival in New York City. Working as a legal researcher, free lance journalist, consumer reporter, part-time muckraker and public speaker, his work has also been featured on Pipeline Internet as part of the weekly *Get-A-Grip* column.

Mr. Alvin (the *Original "Mad as Hell New Yorker"*) has appeared on the *Weekend Today Show* on NBC-TV, *Good Day New York* on the FOX network, *NY-1 News, CBS News Radio* and in the *City Smarts* section of the *New York Daily News.*

He has prevailed over most of the 55 hassles in this book and shares the tips and tactics that have worked for him.

In 1996, *The New York City Get-A-Grip Gripe Book* was honored as one of the 25 Most Outstanding References Books of the Year by the New York Public Library Reference Committee.